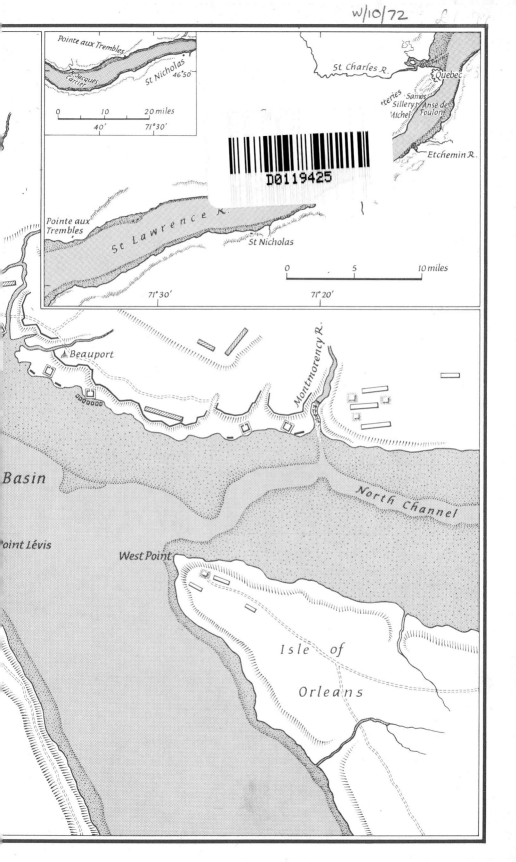

Pointe aux Trembles
St Nicholas 46°50'

0   10   20 miles
40'   71°30'

St Charles R.

Quebec

rteries Samos
Sillery Anse des
Michel Foulon

Etchemin R.

D0119425

Pointe aux
Trembles

St Lawrence R.

St Nicholas

0   5   10 miles

71° 30'   71° 20'

Montmorency R.

Beauport

Basin

North Channel

Point Lévis

West Point

Isle   of

Orleans

£ 2 –

WITH WOLFE TO QUEBEC

February 1973.
fondest love
            Priscilla, Lottie and
                        Luke.

WITH
WOLFE
TO
QUEBEC

The Path to Glory

Seek out – less often sought than found –
A soldier's grave, for thee the best;
Then look around, and choose thy ground,
And take thy rest.

BYRON

OLIVER WARNER

COLLINS

TORONTO AND LONDON

1972

William Collins Sons & Co Ltd
Toronto · London · Glasgow · Sydney
Auckland · Johannesburg

First published 1972
© Oliver Warner 1972

ISBN 1 0 00 211942 0

Set in Monophoto Bembo
de Lange/van Leer NV Amsterdam & Deventer
Made and printed in The Netherlands

TO ÅKE LINDWALL

CONTENTS

MAPS

PART ONE

JAMES WOLFE

New France

James Wolfe · Rochefort · Louisbourg

the Gaspé Expedition

JAMES WOLFE

I

THE magnificence, problems and potentialities of Canada are on a vast scale. This has been evident so long that it requires some effort to imagine how the country appeared to James Wolfe more than two centuries ago. The west was unmapped; the extent of the prairies was unguessed at; whilst those huge territories of the far north were felt to be as forbidding as their climate.

'New France', which was the name by which Canada was then known to Europe, threatening as she seemed to the British colonies of 'New England' further south, was indeed formidable enough, but human beings, even the savage Redskins, were thin on the ground.

Fish and fur had first attracted Europeans to Canada. At the end of the 15th century Cabot, exploring the waters off Cape Breton Island, Nova Scotia and Newfoundland, reported such a wealth of cod that shoals sometimes 'stayed his shippes.' A sea harvest had continued ever since. This became of ever-increasing importance, and was the subject of edicts, regulations and claims on the part of various countries including Spain, Portugal, France and England.

Pioneering journeys by Jacques Cartier, who made formal claim to New France on behalf of his king as early as 1534, were followed up by successors, some of them equally adventurous. By the reign of Henry IV, merchants of Rouen had secured a fur monopoly covering the Canadian trade. In the early years of the 17th century Samuel de Champlain founded Quebec. At first it was a seasonal trading post: permanent settlers came in 1615, among the earliest being Abraham Martin, who became known as a St. Lawrence pilot. Martin cleared and cultivated the stretch of land lying to the west of the later city. This area came to be known, variously, as the Plains or Heights of Abraham.

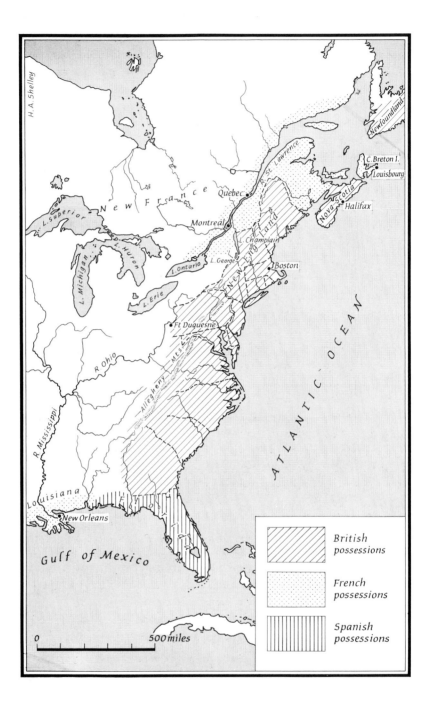

The city which was to become the key to Canada was captured by a small English force in 1629, in the name of Charles I, who held it for three years as a pledge for the unpaid dowry of his French queen, Henrietta Maria.

Louis XIV made Quebec a royal Province at a time when its European inhabitants at last numbered thousands rather than hundreds. It was attacked in 1690 by an expedition from Boston, and threatened in 1711, but both attempts failed.

If French interests had been confined to the north it is possible, though unlikely, that the British colonies of the Atlantic seaboard would have expanded westwards without a fraction of the fighting which marked the earlier decades of the 18th century. But France claimed more. She tried to bar, by the exertions of her own people and with the aid of Indian allies, all extension of British trading and territorial interests beyond the Allegheny Mountains. The range penned in an increasing, vigorous and independent population of farmers and traders, numbering well over a million by 1755.

To the south were the Floridas, which belonged to Spain, and Louisiana, which could have become one of the richer jewels in the French crown, had not France later ceded it to Spain by secret treaty. The French long nourished the idea of a strategic chain of forts stretching from the Gulf of Mexico to the Great Lakes system. If this had ever been realised, it would have encircled the British colonies as effectively as a second mountain range. Although it was a spectacular conception, execution was attempted only spasmodically, and with limited success.

An indication of the pattern of the future was given in 1745, the year before Culloden. This was the capture of the powerful French fortress of Louisbourg, on Cape Breton Island, which in time of war provided a continual threat to British-American sea-borne communications, and was in fact vital in defence or attack. The mainspring of the enterprise had been Governor William Shirley of Massachusetts.

It had at one time been the intention of the British Government to follow up Shirley's initiative with full-scale operations against New France, but these were not attempted. Instead, Louisbourg was handed back to France under the terms of the Treaty of Aix la Chapelle, which was signed in 1748.

American rage and disappointment knew no bounds, and this was entirely justified, for it was plain to anyone living in New England that the work of their soldiers would, some time or other, have to be done all over again. It was intolerable that two great European nations, France and Britain, should strive, generation after generation, for predominance on the eastern seaboard of North America. One of the two would have to take second place, and the Colonists of British North America were resolved it should not be them. American interests had been sacrificed to a temporary and uncertain balance of power in Europe, and as they had not been directly represented at the peace negotiation, they had been unable to make an effective protest.

Fortunately, there was not long to wait before another opportunity occurred to attack New France. Hostilities broke out again in 1756 and were to continue for seven momentous years, which gave the war its name. This time, the resources of the mother country were to be far more seriously engaged in the interests of the Americans. The scene was set for Wolfe's appearance in Canada.

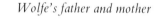

Wolfe's father and mother

An Indian family in Canada

II

James Wolfe, who was destined to make a name for himself both at Louisbourg and Quebec, was a professional soldier in the fullest meaning of the term. He was the son and grandson of officers of the army. From an early age he had followed the drum, not doubting that this was his proper line in life, and determined to succeed in the career of arms.

His family were long settled in Ireland. His grandfather, Edward Wolfe, served under William III, Anne and George I, reached the rank of major, and died in 1715. His father, also named Edward, was born in 1685 and at the age of sixteen was given a commission in a regiment of Marines. He served in Flanders under Marlborough, had become a lieutenant colonel by the age of thirty-two, and died as a lieutenant general in 1759, six months before his elder son.

Edward Wolfe married Henrietta, daughter of Edward Thompson of Long Marston, Yorkshire. He and his wife had two sons, both to become soldiers. James Wolfe was born at Westerham on 2 January 1727, Edward Wolfe a year later. Edward became a lieutenant in the 12th Regiment of Foot, and died on active service in Flanders aged sixteen.

The early 18th century offered many opportunities for campaigners, and youth was no bar to advancement at the front, though the more glittering appointments fell to those of higher status than the Wolfes. James's rise showed this. After some schooling at Greenwich, where his parents then lived, he was appointed second-lieutenant in his father's regiment of Marines at the age of fourteen. He exchanged into the 12th Foot, and in 1742 went across to Ghent for active service against the French in the War of the Austrian Succession.

He was a born soldier. In 1743, when not much over sixteen, he had become adjutant of his battalion. On 12 June he took part in his first battle. It was at Dettingen, where he had a horse shot under him, and where he came under favourable notice of the Duke of Cumberland. A year later he was a substantive captain in the 4th Foot, who were campaigning on the Scheldt. Within twelve months he was serving as a brigade major. He

William, Duke of Cumberland at Culloden

was then sent home to take part against the Jacobite rising under Prince Charles Edward Stuart, the Young Pretender. His father was also with the Government forces for a short time, but saw no fighting.

James Wolfe was at Falkirk and Culloden as ADC to General Hawley. Afterwards he remained in Scotland with his regiment. The settlement of the Highlands was altogether different in spirit from the operations which General Monck had conducted, when left to do a similar job by Oliver Cromwell in the previous century. Wolfe had to be prepared to take women and children as hostages, lay waste the country, burn houses, sieze livestock. Once, at least, he had gone further. He told a brother officer of how he had tried to capture a much-wanted rebel with a detachment deliberately made too small for the purpose. 'I gave the serjeant orders,' so he wrote, 'in case he should succeed, and was attacked by the clan with a view to rescue their chief, to kill him instantly, which I concluded would draw on the destruction of the detachment, and furnish me with sufficient pretext (without waiting for further instructions) to march into their

country where I would have laid about me without compunc-
tion.' He wrote the last few words in idiomatic French, but it
made them no more pleasant.

From Scotland Wolfe returned to the Continent and in
July 1747 was present at the battle of Lauffeld, serving under
General Sir James Mordaunt, who was to be of some importance
in his life. He was wounded, and for the second time received
the thanks of Cumberland for his conduct.

Early in the following year James paid his addresses to
Elizabeth Lawson, a niece of General Mordaunt, who was a Maid
of Honour to the Princess of Wales. He was unlucky in that
neither the lady nor his own parents favoured the match.
Henrietta Wolfe wanted her son to marry a certain Miss
Hoskins, but the girl was of another mind, and became engaged
to John Warde of Squerryes Court, Westerham, the Wardes
and Wolfes being long-standing family friends.

Differences over this choice of possible wives led to a coolness

Elizabeth Lawson

between Wolfe and his parents which, although it did not last long, cannot have been made easier from the fact that Wolfe had an explosive temper. Of this, he later wrote frankly to his mother:

My temper is much too warm, and sudden resentment forces out expressions and even actions that are neither justifiable nor excusable, but you must have observed that people are apt to resent what they take for injuries with more than common quickness when they come from an unexpected quarter. When once I know that people have entertained a very ill opinion I imagine they never change, and though I flatter myself that I have a sense of justice strong enough to keep me from doing wrong, even to an enemy, yet there lurks a hidden poison in the heart . . .

It is my misfortune to catch fire on a sudden, to answer letters the moment I receive them. The next day perhaps would have carried more moderation with it; every ill turn through my whole life has had this haste, and the first impulse of resentment for its true cause, and it proceeds from pride.

This confession is of great importance to the understanding of Wolfe's personality, and it explains some of the difficulties he encountered during his last campaign, particularly among those who did not know him well, or who were not prepared to make allowances.

In general, and despite such set-backs as were to be expected in the career of one who had no powerful influence behind him, Wolfe was content, not with himself, but with his lot in life and with his family. 'Nobody,' he wrote to his father, 'perhaps has more reason to be satisfied with his station and success in the world than myself. Nobody can have better parents, and I have hitherto never wanted friends; but happiness or ease, which is all we can pretend to, lies in the mind or nowhere.'

His passion for self-improvement was ceaseless. It was not every rising officer of Foot who, in his early twenties, would engage a tutor in mathematics, and another in Latin, and slave away so hard that, as he reported, the hours of toil 'have not even left me with the qualities of a coxcomb; for I can neither laugh nor sing, nor talk an hour upon nothing. The latter is a sensible loss, for it excludes a gentleman from all good company, and makes him extremely unfit for the conversation of the polite world.'

Not long after writing this, Wolfe spent a happy interlude of leave in Paris, where he did his best to master colloquial French, and in time came to speak it with ease. There he was given a view of the world which extended far beyond the confines of military camps and garrison society. Looking at mankind in general, and at the French and English in particular, he was moved to note:

There are men that only desire to shine, and that had rather say a smart thing than do a great one; there are others – rare birds – that had rather be than seem to be. Of the first kind this country is a well stored magazine; of the second, our own has some few examples.

Wolfe's rise as a soldier would in some later periods have seemed spectacular, though it never appeared so to himself. He had become a substantive major in the 20th Foot by the age of twenty-two, with the acting rank of lieutenant-colonel. He was confirmed in his acting rank in March 1750. This was much faster promotion than his father had received, but James Wolfe

Paris at the time of Wolfe's visit

had seen much fighting. He was with his regiment, often in Scotland, until the outbreak of the Seven Years War in 1756.

What anyone, not of his immediate family, actually knew about Wolfe at this time must have been strictly limited. Even today, there are certain disadvantages which an enquirer who wishes to acquaint himself as fully as possible with the outline of his life is compelled to accept, since they cannot be overcome. The fact that he died at the age of thirty two, and that his biography was not attempted on any scale until Robert Wright published a life in 1864, more than half a century after the principal survivors of his campaigns had passed away, are the two main handicaps. On the other hand, the circumstances of his final battle made him so quickly and permanently into a national hero, that his apotheosis has a momentum and an interest of its own which is exceptional. Moreover, his sudden fame led to the preservation of letters and documents associated with him which, considering all the circumstances, are respectable in extent.

The greatest gaps are the most private. This is natural enough, if only through the wish of those who were most nearly linked with him to keep his memory bright. But certain areas of ignorance, of which there are a good many, can be filled in only by speculation with little or no supporting evidence, and of all aspects of pseudo-biography, this is surely one of the most to be deplored.

Allowing that to be so, it is likely that a young man strictly brought up, with a very formidable mother, pitched into warfare and into arduous responsibility while still in his teens, and soldiering in uncongenial, sometimes barren places year after year, would cut loose. It is known that he did so, once at least, in London, but this may have been too near home, and there are indications that he found most relaxation during a visit to Ireland in 1752, where he went on leave. In that country he felt very much at ease: and there he had an appreciative and hospitable relation in his uncle, Major Walter Wolfe.

One scrap of support exists for the notion that Wolfe formed some sort of attachment in Ireland, possibly of a not very creditable sort. One of his officers at Quebec, who had made himself notorious long before he ever served with Wolfe for a series of drawings making fun of his superiors, produced one relating Wolfe to an 'Irish Venus' which has caused some perplexity ever since. The implication was that someone of the opposite sex would be distressed to hear of Wolfe's death. The point of the cartoon would have rested on the knowledge that Wolfe, despite the fact that he was by that time betrothed to a lady in fashionable society, had thoughts elsewhere, and must have expressed them so freely that they had become fairly common knowledge. This had nothing to do with his soldiering, but it does indicate that Wolfe had the normal appetites of his age, and that he may sometimes have indulged them.

By the age of thirty, he could consider himself seasoned, far more so than most of his contemporaries. He had been present at four full-scale battles and a score of lesser engagements; he had trained his regiment to a point of efficiency which was handsomely acknowledged by his superiors, and he had taken note of how independent command should be exercised. Willing to learn and eager to lead, Wolfe now only awaited the

The Irish Venus mourning General Wolfe —

Townshend's cartoon of Wolfe's 'Irish Venus'

right opportunity to show his capacity.

In the earlier months of 1757, shortly after the outbreak of the Seven Years War, the question of further promotion came up. This was one of extreme importance professionally, since the step in rank between lieutenant-colonel and full colonel was significant beyond the ordinary. A lieutenant-colonel saw to the training and administration of a regiment, but in the case of a full colonel, the unit belonged to him in a very practical sense, and it bore his name. Yet regular duties were neither entailed nor expected, and it was almost like a piece of property, to be 'managed' by subordinates if, as was the rule, the colonel so desired.

When it came to the point, George II, in whose hands decision lay, announced that he thought Wolfe too young for a full colonelcy. However, Wolfe may have found consolation in that he was now ordered to take part in the first of the three combined operations of his career – an expedition against Rochefort.

George II at Dettingen

III

Of the three combined operations in which Wolfe took part, Rochefort in 1757, Louisbourg in 1758, and Quebec the year following, the one to Rochefort taught him much. It also cemented certain friendships which were to be useful to him in the future.

During the Seven Years War, Britain's Continental ally was Prussia, and it was in the interests of her king, Frederick the Great, that Pitt, by whose masterful hands the country's strategy was guided, planned a series of descents on the coast of France. These were intended to divert a far larger proportion of French resources than was warranted by the forces deployed against them. A few were successful, and in sum they were about as effective as the operation of the regular British army based on the Continent, which was not saying much. They did less for the allied cause than subsidies in cash, which were another means of helping Prussia.

When engaged in war across the Channel, George II, being Elector of Hanover as well as King of England, focussed his attention on the interests of his German patrimony. Pitt, whose view was world wide, favoured the use of his country's naval power where it could be most effective – on the far side of the Atlantic, and in the East, particularly in India. If Rochefort was intended to help Prussia, Louisbourg and Quebec were part of a grand plan not only to relieve pressure on the American colonists, but to attack France overseas, where she was thought to be most vulnerable.

It was Horace Walpole, that invaluable gossip, who pinpointed certain characteristics of the Rochefort commanders. Mordaunt, he said, 'had once been remarkable for alertness and bravery, but was much broken in spirit and constitution.' He was also incorrigibly pessimistic, a sin in any leader, young or old, military or civil. Pitt had intended Major General Henry Seymour Conway for chief place, but he was not favoured either by the King or by his army contemporaries. Walpole said he 'had a natural indecision in his temper, weighing with

William Pitt in about 1754

Sir Edward Hawke

too much minuteness . . . whatever depended on his own judgement.' In fairness to Mordaunt, Conway felt as doubtful about the whole project as anyone concerned with it. That being so, it was a pity that Mordaunt and Conway were not left behind, and the command given to Wolfe, who was to be quartermaster general.

In considering Wolfe, the tone of Walpole's comment rose appreciably. Here, he said, was 'a young officer who had contracted a reputation from his intelligence of discipline, and from the perfection to which he had brought his regiment. The world could not expect more from him than he thought himself capable of performing. He looked upon danger as the favourable moment that would call forth all his talents.'

Wolfe had a counterpart in enterprise, ability and professional mastery in a sea officer serving under Hawke who in due time was to adorn every rank in the Navy. This was Captain the

Honourable Richard Howe,* commanding the *Magnanime*, a ship of the line taken from the French nine years earlier. She was known for being one of the smartest in the Service. 'Howe,' said Walpole, 'was undaunted as a rock, and as silent; the characteristics of his whole race. He and Wolfe contracted a friendship like the union of cannon and gunpowder.'

There was a young guards officer on Conway's staff, also well known to Wolfe, whose name was William Hamilton. He had been present at Lauffeld and had later spent some time with Wolfe in Paris on furlough. Hamilton was younger than Wolfe and below him in rank, but the two were attracted to one another. 'If I can be of the least use to him,' wrote Wolfe in a letter home about his friend, 'I shall not neglect the opportunity.'

Ironically, it was Hamilton who was to be of service to Wolfe's fame, for in due time the younger man became Sir William Hamilton, K.B., for over thirty years Minister to the Court of Naples, the husband of Emma, and the friend of Nelson. Hamilton's enthusiasm for Wolfe was a stimulus to the admiration which Nelson had always felt for the soldier, and he provided a personal link between two exemplars of valour. Hamilton also afforded a remarkable glimpse of General Conway's odd irresponsibility. He told Horace Walpole that while on the Rochefort expedition Conway 'was so careless and so fearless as to be trying a burning glass on a bomb, yes, a bomb, the match of which had been cut short to prevent its being fired by accidental sparks.' Hamilton snatched the glass from Conway's hand 'before he had at all thought what it was all about!'

The expedition sailed, arrived and deliberated. There was, however, one sparkling exception to the dithering which characterised the whole affair. This was Howe's example in the

---

* Howe had an elder and a younger brother, both soldiers. The elder, the third Viscount Howe, was already well known to Wolfe from his active service reputation. 'The noblest Englishman that has appeared in my time,' he said, 'and the best soldier in the army.' He was in Canada, but was to be killed in a skirmish with the French and their Indian allies at Trout Brook, Lake George, before another year was out, his title going to his naval brother. The younger, William Howe, was to be with Wolfe at Louisbourg and Quebec, and to win his approbation. Serving in the *Magnanime* under Richard Howe was a lieutenant, James Chads, on whom Wolfe was to rely during the approach to his last battle.

Magnanime, which, in the words of Rodney, who was also present, 'gained him the universal applause of both army and navy.'

The key defences of Rochefort were the batteries mounted on the Ile d'Aix in the Basque Road. Hawke ordered a naval bombardment. Howe took the leading part, silently sailing in, disdaining to answer French fire until he was close upon the principal fort. A description by an eye-witness states that:

Before the attack began, Captain Howe received the fire of the garrison with great intrepidity, ordered all his men to lay down upon the decks, turned all his live cattle, fowls and unnecessaries overboard; himself only with his speaking trumpet in his hand, the pilot and the man at the helm appearing on deck, till he came within sixty yards of the bastions, when he began so furious a fire that the Monsieurs said that something more than a man must be on board that ship: the men in the garrison were so much terrified that most of them clapped themselves down under the works and in the ditches, nor could be prevailed upon to stand to their guns, which obliged the Governor to strike the colours, and was no sooner done than they all jumped up, taking snuff, dancing and rejoicing, as if they had gained a victory.

With naval parties landed on the Ile d'Aix (one of them included Wolfe), an energetic commander would at once have pressed his advantage and gone on in to Rochefort. But although the French were in fact both weak in numbers, ill-organised, and alarmed by the size of the expedition, the chance was missed. An opportunity which could well have been turned into success in the tradition of Drake was allowed to go by default. It is hard not to believe that any foray commanded by Mordaunt would have ended the same miserable way.

Wolfe, who not only prospected the Ile d'Aix but thereafter put forward a detailed tactical plan for a follow-up, wrote bitterly on his return home that on 25 September, the day of greatest opportunity, a Council of War 'sat from morning till late at night... The result of the debates was unanimously not to attack the place they were ordered to attack, and for reasons that no soldier will allow to be sufficient.' Needless to say, Wolfe was not a member of the Council; nor was Howe. He added: 'if they would even blunder on and fight a little, making some

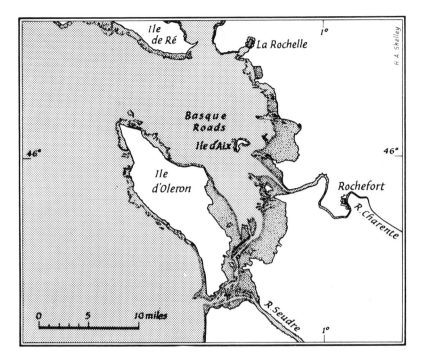

ameids to the Public by their courage for their want of skill –
but this excessive degree of caution, or whatever name it
deserves, leaves exceeding bad impression among the troops,
who, to do them justice, upon this occasion showed all the signs
of spirit and good will.' The patient rank and file had seen what
a single ship could achieve. Why should they not have felt
confidence in success?

Wolfe summed up his feelings about combined operations in
passages which have since become well-known, and which have
lost nothing of their relevance for the grim study of war. To his
father he wrote:

We have lost the lucky moment in war and are not able to recover it.
The whole expedition has not cost the nation ten men; nor has any
man been able to distinguish himself in the service of his country,
except Mr. Howe, who was an example to us all.

'The lucky moment in war' was a phrase which showed how
well Wolfe understood the history of the profession of arms. To
a brother officer, Captain William Rickson, he opened his mind
in more detail.

I have found out that an admiral should endeavour to run into an enemy's port immediately after he appears before it; that he should anchor the transport ships and frigates as close as can be to the land; that he should reconnoitre and observe it as quick as possible, and lose no time in getting the troops on shore; that previous directions should be given in respect to land the troops, and a proper disposition made for the boats of all sorts, appointing leaders and fit persons for conducting the different divisions.

So much for the naval side. The remarks were not altogether fair to Hawke, who had anticipated many of Wolfe's requirements. As for the soldiers:

. . . experience shows me that, in an affair depending upon vigour and despatch, the generals should settle their plan of operations, so that no time may be lost in idle debate and consultations when the sword should be drawn; that pushing on smartly is the road to success, and more particularly so in an affair of this nature; that nothing is to be reckoned an obstacle to your undertaking which is not found really so upon *tryal*; that in war something must be allowed to chance and fortune, seeing it is in its nature hazardous, and an option of difficulties; that the greatness of an object should come under consideration, opposed to the impediments that lie in the way; that the honour of one's country is to have some weight, and that, in particular circumstances and times the loss of 1000 men is rather an advantage to a nation than otherwise, seeing that gallant attempts raise its reputation and make it respectable; whereas the contrary appearances sink the credit of a country, ruin the troops, and create infinite uneasiness and discontent at home.

Fortunately, by the autumn, the old king who had led his troops in person at Dettingen and who loved the soldier's trade, had learnt of Wolfe's zeal at Rochefort and had second thoughts about his promotion.

On 21st October Wolfe was able to write to his father from Blackheath: '. . . the King has been pleased to give me the rank of Colonel which at this time is more to be prized than any other, because it carries with it a favourable appearance of my conduct upon this late expedition, and an acceptance of my good intentions.'

Surprisingly, by Wolfe's own account, he owed his step in rank, in part at least, to naval recommendation, and that from the highest quarters. 'I am something indebted to Sir Edward Hawke,' so he told his father, 'for having spoken to Lord Anson, who took the trouble to repeat it to the King.'

Anson was at the time First Lord of the Admiralty. His opinion, and that of Hawke, must have widely differed from that of some of Wolfe's contemporaries. For when, at a later stage in his life, Wolfe had been nominated for independent command, and there were protests that he was mad, the King is reported to have barked: 'Mad, is he? Then I wish he would *bite* some of my other generals!'

George II was not an endearing character, but some sterling appointments should be remembered in his favour. Years earlier, when Hawke was still a captain, the King had refused, against advice, to have him shelved. Hawke lived to add the sea victory of Quiberon Bay to the 'Wonderful Year' of 1759. It was appropriate that no less a man should have spoken up for Wolfe.

IV

If Quebec was the key to Canada, the French fortress at Louisbourg, on the coast of Cape Breton Island, was the key to Quebec. Today, Louisbourg has well restored signs of former grandeur. Once it was the strongest naval and military base in New France, a threat to unfriendly shipping plying the North Atlantic. In the mid-18th century its menace was such that its very existence prompted the foundation of Halifax, Nova Scotia, as an opposing stronghold.

Pitt had planned an attack on Louisbourg for the summer of the Rochefort fiasco, but this idea had come to nothing. A year which had begun with the disgrace of the shooting of Admiral Byng for failing to relieve Minorca, ended the way it deserved, in reverse and discouragement.

1758, so Pitt was determined, should be different.

The planned descent on Louisbourg was the most important part of a threefold strategic design on the French position in Canada and America.

Brigadier John Forbes, who had once commanded the Scots

Greys, was to attempt the second part, the capture of Fort Duquesne and the recovery of the valley of the Ohio, which had been lost in previous operations. Although he was over sixty, Forbes had developed a talent for colonial warfare, which in general was campaigning fitted for younger men.

The third great aim was to recover the line of Lakes George and Champlain, and to penetrate by that route as far as possible towards Montreal and Quebec. This venture was entrusted to General James Abercromby. He was a bad choice, Pitt's one serious mistake in the higher appointments. Even so, had not Howe – his second-in-command – been killed by a stray bullet, it is possible that matters would have fared better with Abercromby than they did.

Louisbourg would tax the best commanders, and the Minister made no mistake. For the naval part he chose the Honourable Edward Boscawen, a favourite with Hawke. His father was Lord Falmouth and his grandmother, Arabella Churchill, was Marlborough's sister, and at one time a mistress of James II. Boscawen was an admiral of the Blue. He had already commanded on the North American Station, and was known to the lower deck as 'Old Dreadnought', or, more surreptitiously, 'Wry-necked Dick' from the queer way he would cock his head. The sailors loved him. So did Wolfe. 'We all have the utmost confidence in Admiral Boscawen's zeal and activity in the service,' he wrote, 'and when we heard he was to command the fleet we assured ourselves that the campaign would be vigorous and active.'

Boscawen chose a highly intelligent wife, Frances Granville. Years later, after a particularly delightful party given by Mrs Garrick, which included Mrs Boscawen, Hannah More, Sir Joshua Reynolds, Dr Burney, historian of music, and Samuel Johnson, Boswell was moved to whisper to Mrs Boscawen: 'I believe this is as much as can be made of life.'

Boscawen was forty-seven. Major-General Jeffrey Amherst, who was to command the troops, was six years younger, and again a wise selection. His military method was to hasten slowly, and he lacked Wolfe's fire, but he was as good a choice as the army offered within his particular seniority, and in due time he rose to peerage and the rank of field marshal. A guards-

Admiral Boscawen

man of much battle experience, who had at one time served on the staff of Lord Ligonier, Pitt's principal military adviser, Amherst soon learnt to respect Wolfe, even if he did not always agree with him. His own great strength was in co-ordination and administration.

As Louisbourg was regarded as the most hopeful undertaking of the three, fourteen regular battalions, numbering over 11,000 men, were at first assigned, and they were to have the fullest support from Boscawen's fleet. If the fortress fell early enough in the year, an immediate advance was to be made upon Quebec by way of the St. Lawrence, and the operation can, therefore, be

Wolfe by Brigadier Townshend, 1759

thought of as the essential preliminary to Wolfe's last campaign. If success were to be delayed until late in the season, the commanders were to turn their attention to the minor French settlements on the Canadian coast, and perhaps to Louisiana.

In January sixteen ships of the line and attendant frigates were ordered to be made ready for Boscawen. Seven others had wintered at Halifax, and the total numbers available would, so Pitt judged, give Boscawen powerful superiority over anything the French were likely to muster for the protection of Louisbourg. Rear Admiral Sir Charles Hardy was to sail at once for Halifax in the *Royal William* to establish a preliminary blockade. Commodore Philip Durell was also to sail early in the year with drafts for the troops at New York and Halifax, his pendant flying in the *Princess Amelia*.

In the upshot, there were long delays, mainly due to weather. Amherst himself took passage in the *Dublin*, a new 74-gun ship commanded by Captain Rodney, who was to become famous for his part in the War of American Independence later in the century. It was a stroke of luck for Rodney that, when six days from home and off the French coast, he met with and captured the Indiaman *Montmartel*, which was loaded with coffee and other valuable cargo from the Isle of Bourbon. It was characteristic that he considered his prize before his important passenger. He put into the neutral port of Vigo, where by good luck the *Peregrine* sloop of war was met with. Her captain was ordered to take the *Montmartel* back to England, and the voyage proceeded. One way and another, it had cost a fortnight's delay, and although Amherst did not complain, he wrote to Pitt expressing the hope that the latter part of the voyage would be more expeditious. In this he was to be disappointed. Calms, then storms and fogs held up the *Dublin* to such an extent that the general was seventy-two days on passage.

Wolfe was to be one of three brigadiers, the others being Charles Lawrence, Governor of Novia Scotia, and Edward Whitmore, who was at the head of the New York contingent. The colonels included the Honourable James Murray, who had been at Rochefort and who was to be at Quebec. The acting lieutenant colonels included the Honourable William Howe of the 58th Foot, who had to wait over a year for confirmation of rank.

General Amherst

Howe had served under Wolfe in the 20th Regiment and learnt so well that Wolfe reported him to be 'at the head of the best-trained battalion in all America.' This was, perhaps, a pardonable partiality.

Wolfe sailed with Admiral Boscawen in the *Namur*. 'From Christopher Columbus's time to our own days,' he wrote home, 'there perhaps has never been a more extraordinary voyage. The continual opposition of contrary winds, calms or currents baffled all our skill and wore out all our patience. A fleet of men-of-war well-manned, unencumbered with transports, commanded by an officer of the first reputation, has been eleven weeks in its passage.'

Wolfe was a bad sailor, and the voyage would have given him a shrewd idea of some of the difficulties with which seamen had to contend. During his weeks at sea he had been working on a plan to use the flexibility conferred by superior sea power to land in various places on Cape Breton Island, and to attack Louisbourg indirectly. If anything had happened to Amherst he might have been able to carry it out, but after the general had at last been united with his army it was soon made clear that originality was not among Amherst's more prominent qualities. He favoured what Wolfe considered an all too orthodox plan of attack. It wholly lacked flexibility or the characteristic of surprise. For the troops were to land in Gaburus Bay, due west of Louisbourg – just exactly where they were expected!

The decision nearly led to disaster. The boats approached the shore at a place where the French were well entrenched, and although the troops were covered by fire from the ships, the enemy withheld their own until the assault was close inshore, when they opened up with appalling effect. Wolfe, who was in the leading flight, at first saw little for it but a withdrawal, but two subalterns discovered a stretch of beach which was masked from the entrenchments. Wolfe, following up their initiative, got most of his men ashore, though some boats were swamped or smashed against the rocks and many were drowned in the surf.

Once on shore, Wolfe was at his best. Anticipating an attack in the open by grenadiers hurrying from the entrenchments, he made his men, though shaken and disorganised by their boat journey, stand their ground. When the French appeared, they were driven back. Lawrence brought his division ashore in support, and within minutes the defenders, seeing their retreat threatened, broke for the town, leaving Wolfe in possession. 'It may be said,' he wrote to his uncle in Ireland, Major Walter Wolfe, 'that we made a rash and ill-advised attempt to land, and by the greatest of good fortune imaginable we succeeded.' He had turned what looked like being a bloody repulse into a triumph.

Such was the superiority in numbers and in supplies of Amherst and Boscawen, and such the success of the opening moves that the ultimate fate of Louisbourg was now certain. The most the French could hope for was to impose delay.

The immediate problem before the besiegers was to subdue the forts commanding the harbour, of which there were two, the Batterie Royale, which the French obligingly abandoned,

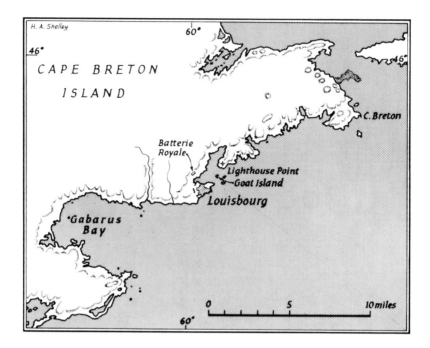

60°

46°

CAPE BRETON

ISLAND

C. Breton

Batterie
Royale

Lighthouse Point
Goat Island

Louisbourg

Gabarus
Bay

0   5   10 miles

60°

and another on Goat Island, at the entrance, which was soon
pounded to rubble by mortar fire. That difficulty over, there
remained the French ships sheltering under and supporting the
fortress guns of Louisbourg itself.

For the weather which had hampered the British fleet had
enabled ships to elude the blockade of the French ports. Hawke
had not allowed anything to leave Rochefort, which at the
time was the main centre of supplies for Canada, but the Marquis
Charry des Gouttes, who had been chosen for the Louisbourg
naval command, got away from Brest in the 74-gun *Prudent*. He
was followed by Captain Beaussier de l'Isle in another ship of
the line, with which he escorted three vessels carrying stores and
a regular battalion of infantry. His passage took only twenty-
four days. Later still two more ships of war and four transports
got away under the Comte du Chaffault de Besné with more
stores and a further battalion for Canada. Hardy, on the other
side of the Atlantic, was driven off station by the same bad
weather which enabled the French to evade his watch, and by
the time he could return, des Gouttes and his captains were snug

at anchor under the fortifications. The total French force, including ships which had wintered in Canada, was thirteen, of which five were of the line.

Wolfe's follow-up was to march his brigade round the harbour to seize Lighthouse Point, on the side of the harbour opposite the town. He established mortar or what were then called bomb batteries as he went, and these were armed direct from the fleet. By 18 June, ten days after the landing, all was ready for Wolfe to bombard the harbour and its shipping. Fire began the next night, and although Wolfe was disappointed at the performance of the artillerymen, des Gouttes was soon in despair. He begged the Governor's leave to try to break out with his squadron, but permission was refused. The ships, so it was argued, were too valuable for the defence of the town.

Boscawen, deprived of the immediate prospect of a sea fight, and unwilling to take his ships into the harbour in the face of the Louisbourg fortress guns, re-inforced by those of the French man-of-war, served for a time on shore.

Wolfe wrote to Lord George Sackville:

The Admiral and General have carried on public service with great harmony, industry and union. Mr. Boscawen has given all and even more than we could ask of him. He has furnished arms and ammunition, pioneers, sappers, miners, gunners, carpenters, boats, and is, I must confess, no bad *fantassin* himself and an excellent backhand at a siege.

Sir Charles Hardy too in particular, and all the Officers of the Navy in general, have given us their utmost assistance and with the greatest cheerfulness imaginable. I have been often in pain for Sir Charles's squadron at an anchor off the harbour's mouth. They rid out some very hard gales of wind rather than leave an opening for the French to escape.

This was a very different atmosphere from that at Rochefort the year before, and Boscawen, when he exchanged the role of foot soldier for his more normal one, surprised everyone by the daring stroke which completed the destruction of the French squadron.

Matters were begun on 21 July by a bomb which fell on the poop of the French *Célèbre*. Within a few minutes she, and two ships near her, were blazing. A storm of shot and shell was

Attack on the French ships at Louisbourg

concentrated on the burning mass, and in the end only des Goutte's flagship and the *Bienfaisant* could be saved. They, however, continued to be used with great effect, and Boscawen resolved to cut them out from under the French batteries.

On the night of 25 July a flotilla was organised in two divisions, commanded by Captains Laforey and Balfour at the head of 600 seamen. Under cover of darkness and the fire of every gun and mortar in the British lines, the vessels were seized by boat parties and made prize. The *Bienfaisant*, as soon as her cables were cut, took the ground and had to be burnt, but in the light of the flames the sailors towed off the flagship, anchoring her on the far side of the harbour. It was a blow which struck deeply at the spirit of resistance, and when Boscawen threatened to take his fleet in, capitulation followed. 3,000 soldiers were made prisoner of war, and the French naval squadron was wiped out. The state of des Gouttes's force is revealing. He had 135 officers and 1,124 seamen fit for duty, but a further 1,347 were in hospital, an indication of the toll of sickness and the ardours of the siege.

At first Amherst and Wolfe were for pressing on to Quebec, but Boscawen demurred. The season was becoming late. The transports, riding out gales at their indifferent anchorage in Gabarus Bay, had lost most of their ground tackle; provisions were running short in the fleet, and there were nearly 5,000 prisoners to embark.

Then, on 31 July, three days after the capitulation, news came which removed any doubts the soldiers may have had as to whether the admiral was right. Abercromby had failed before Ticonderoga. He was believed to be in retreat, in spite of his considerable numbers, and if that were so, New York might be open to a counter stroke. In the circumstances, the most that could be done was to lay waste the nearest French coastal settlements, and to arrange measures of relief for a general who, though incompetent, proved to be in no danger.

To set against Abercromby's failure there were items of cheering news to round off the taking of Louisbourg. Although Abercromby had not felt himself strong enough, after his repulse, to renew an attack on the French, he was persuaded by one of his lieutenant colonels, John Bradstreet, to let him strike out to the west and attempt the destruction of Fort Frontenac, at the eastern entrance to Lake Ontario.

To New France, Frontenac was a point of strategic importance second only to Louisbourg itself. Not only was it the main depot for the supply of Upper Canada, and of the Ohio forts, but it was also the base from which the French had commanded the great inland waters.

It was at Oswego, on the south eastern shore of Lake Ontario that Bradstreet, with a picked force, launched *bateaux* and whalers. Frontenac was surprised while thinly held, and when a relieving force from Montreal was still far away. It capitulated at once. The captors found a stock of furs and supplies of immense value, and in the harbour there were nine vessels, mounting 100 guns between them. These were carried off or destroyed, and the fort was obliterated. The action, brilliant in execution, restored British command of the Great Lake system, and virtually severed Montreal and Quebec from Upper Canada and the Ohio Valley.

A few days later Forbes took Fort Duquesne, and raised a new structure on the old site. This he named Pittsburgh, in honour of the mainspring of the war.

V

For Wolfe personally, for Sir Charles Hardy and some detachments from the army, there was a post-script to the siege of Louisbourg which was of some significance for the future. Late in August, Amherst sailed south with six regiments, to reinforce Abercromby. Small expeditions were sent to reduce the French settlements round the Bay of Fundy and on Prince Edward Island. Wolfe, with three regiments, four light guns and two howitzers was ordered on other business, the chief of which was to investigate the approaches to the St Lawrence, and to raid such settlements as were within range.

Hardy, who had done so well during the investment of Louisbourg, was given a sizeable little fleet to look after, and this seems to have made him more hesitant than was his way when not in chief command. The regiments took up six

A landing on Cape Breton Island

transports. Hardy also had six ships of the line to protect them, and there was a frigate and a fire-ship under his charge.

On 4 September the squadron anchored in Gaspé Bay, at at the eastern extremity of the peninsula of that name. Wolfe landed with a party of troops, the town of Gaspé was occupied, and the neighbouring country was searched for inhabitants and property. This was work of simple and unopposed destruction, distasteful to disciplined men. They seized 250 small fishing boats, burnt a number of houses, destroyed 6,000 quintals of fish, and carried off thirty seven prisoners, including a woman and child.

Murray, who was with Wolfe, was then sent off with a detachment of Miramachi, which is now in New Brunswick. There he was the means of further destruction. Other forays

Miramachi

were sent against the settlements of Grand' Riviere on the Baie de Chaleur. Most enterprising of all was a party which went to Mont Louis, on the St Lawrence, proceeding along the shore by regular marches. At Mont Louis the usual burning and destruction took place, but at least it yielded some military stores – six guns, a barrel of gunpowder, four barrels of musket-balls, two drums and a pair of colours. It was not very glorious, but it seemed more to the point than operations against fisher-folk who at the best of times lived a hard enough existence.

It was the Mont Louis party which learnt that the French admiral du Chaffault was even then sailing down the river with six ships of the line, two frigates and a few merchantmen. They were bound for France by way of the Straits of Belle Isle. What a chance, thought Wolfe, for a battle between naval forces of equal strength, in which he did not doubt that British training would prove superior. Hardy was less enthusiastic. He did cruise for a few days between Gaspé and the island of Anticosti: but he seemed nervous of the St Lawrence and, at about the time when du Chaffault might have been expected, he returned to Gaspé Bay, where he stayed until all the regiments had been safely re-embarked. Then the whole force sailed away, reaching Louisbourg on 30 September. There would be no more campaigning that year.

'We have done a great deal of mischief,' wrote Wolfe to Amherst, 'spread the terror of his Majesty's arms through the whole gulf, but have added nothing to the reputation of them.' This was plain truth. He hinted that the Navy had not given him all the support possible, declaring that the equipment provided had been 'very improper for the business.' The main ground of complaint seems to have been the lack of small boats. Very little if any new knowledge had been acquired about the navigability of the Lower St Lawrence. Although the bays of Gaspé and Miramichi had been fairly thoroughly explored, the value of such work would be marginal if, as was to be expected, a serious attack on Quebec by the river route was the next objective.

Although the Gaspé expedition was not a pleasant task from any point of view, it is not to be supposed that Wolfe considered it unjustifiable or unnecessary. It was the triviality of the task which disgusted him. He never had the slightest misgivings about treating war as war, and this applied as much to people as to operations. On the very day after the surrender of Louisbourg he wrote home:

I went into Louisbourg this morning to pay my devoirs to the ladies, but found them all so pale and thin with long confinement in a case-ment, that I made my visit very short. The poor women have been heartily frightened, as well they might; but no real harm, either during the siege or after it, has befallen any. A day or two more, and they would have been entirely at our disposal. I was determined to save as many lives, and prevent as much violence as I could, because I am sure such a step would be very acceptable to you and very becoming.

That was Wolfe's whole attitude in a nut-shell, and it was expressed, as so often, to his mother, who must have gained an understanding of war from her elder son rarely equalled among her sex. Wolfe wanted no avoidable bloodshed, and he was glad the ladies were safe. But – if Louisbourg had been stormed, the women to whom he had been so considerate 'would have been entirely at our disposal.' That followed as a matter of course, though it was seldom put quite so bluntly.

Wolfe sailed home in the *Namur* with Admiral Boscawen, and it was Boscawen, not Hardy, who encountered the French. His ships had at the time been scattered by one of those gales which had signalised a very rough season, and he was in inferior force. To Boscawen, this did not signify, and he gave chase at once. A distant brush took place in heavy weather, the only result of which was the recapture of a British East Indiaman. Towards the end of her passage, one of du Chaffault's ships, the *Belliqueux* of 64 guns, was snapped up by Captain Thomas Saumarez of the *Antelope*. The Frenchman sailed right up to Lundy Island, in the Bristol Channel, under the delusion that Brest, his destination, lay just ahead.

It was in this fashion that 1758 came to an end, so far as the trans-Atlantic campaign was concerned. The French had made a notable resistance but, except at Ticonderoga, they had failed everywhere, though they had imposed delay. Canada was hemmed in from east and west. She was being served as her leading men would have served the British colonies of North America. Even so, while Quebec and Montreal remained in French hands, there was a great deal still to do.

PART TWO

BEFORE QUEBEC

*Preparations in England · Saunders's Fleet
Wolfe's Army · The French Command · Vaudreuil and
Montcalm · Saunders sets sail · Bougainville's return
Wolfe's arrival · Cook and the St Lawrence*

BEFORE QUEBEC

I

WHEN Wolfe landed at Portsmouth from the *Namur* he learnt that his regiment, the 67th Foot, was at Salisbury, and it was there that he went at once. He had, however, sent in an application for leave, and this was granted. By 17 November he was at Blackheath with his parents, and very glad his mother must have been to see him, for his father was in the earlier stages of his last illness.

Not a great deal is known about Henrietta Wolfe, but that she was a predominating influence in her son's life is probable. With his father Wolfe appears always to have been on easy, affectionate terms. As fellow soldiers they would have had so much in common that there could never have been any difficulty in communication. Edward Wolfe had none of his son's brilliance, but that he was a highly capable officer is proved by his appointments.

Henrietta Wolfe was a woman who liked her own way so much that she tolerated any breath of opposition with ill grace. This had already been shown in her son's affairs of the heart, and it was to occur again. Not long after he arrived home, Wolfe seems to have been reproached by Pitt for leaving the North American Station, though orders to stay there had in fact never reached him. After writing an explanation to the Minister, Wolfe returned briefly to Salisbury, said farewell to his officers and men, whom he found in excellent shape, and then went by post-chaise to Bath.

In Society, he now found himself something of a lion. His conduct before Louisbourg had been much noticed, and for the first time in his life he enjoyed a touch of popularity, even of fame. He took lodgings in Queen Square, 'to be more at leisure,' as he put it, 'more in the air, and nearer the country.' During the winter months, Bath, which was then in its hey-day,

Queen's Square, Bath, in the eighteength century

attracted the best people, and among them were the Lowther family, including Sir James, afterwards Earl of Lonsdale, and his sister Katherine. Their father had been Governor of Barbados, and James, who was then beginning a Parliamentary career, was one day to prove himself a cunning hand at electioneering.

Wolfe had met Katherine Lowther the previous winter, and their acquaintance blossomed so quickly that they became engaged. Katherine was good looking, and her family were not disposed to object to a man who promised to become a renowned general officer. The chief obstacle to the course of love was Henrietta Wolfe, whose capacity for causing unpleasantness had increased with years and practice. What she had against Katherine, who belonged to one of the most influential families in the north of England, has not been discovered, but jealousy was an obvious ingredient in the situation. That her hostility was strong is, however, evident from a letter which Katherine wrote to her after hearing of Wolfe's death. It is likely that her anger was redoubled when she realised that her son this time meant to disregard her feelings. The engagement does not seem to have been publicly announced, though it was not kept secret. The pair exchanged portraits and gave each other presents. Wolfe wore Katherine's miniature on his last campaign, after which it was returned to her set in diamonds that his estate could not afford.

Wolfe's letters to Katherine no longer exist, and Mrs Wolfe's dislike can be put down only to prejudice. This is sad, for the proof that Wolfe valued and respected his mother lies in the fact that he wrote many of his most prescient letters to her. In them, he treated her as equal and confidant, and he must have felt her to be so.

On the other hand, Wolfe had had much to put up with, and this began very early in his life. There exists a receipt which Henrietta Wolfe used as a 'sovereign remedy for affections of the Chest' which shows a belief, positively mediaeval in spirit, in the most extraordinary ingredients.

Take a peck of green garden snails, wash them in beer, put them in an oven and let them stay till they're done crying; then with a knife and fork prick the green from them, and beat the snail shells and all

Katherine Lowther

in a stone mortar. Then take a quart of green earth-worms, slice them through the middle and strew them with salt: then wash them and beat them, the pot being first put into the still with two handfulls of angelica, a quart of rosemary flowers, then the snails and worms, the agrimony, bear's feet, red dock roots, barberry brake, bilberry, wormwood, of each two handfulls: one handfull of rue, turmeric, and one ounce of saffron, well dried and beaten. Then pour in three gallons of milk. Wait till morning, then put in three ounces of cloves (well beaten), hartshorn, grated. Keep the still covered all night. This done, stir it not. Distil with a moderate fire. The patient must take two spoonfulls at a time.

This perhaps tells us as much about Henrietta Wolfe as a score of letters. As one of her son's biographers wrote: 'He was doubtless made to swallow gallons of this brew, so that his subsequent indifference to the risks and horrors of war needs no explanation.'

So far as those 'risks and horrors' were concerned, there was no question where Wolfe's preferences now lay. He would have wished to return to the Continent, to the kind of campaigning he knew best. There, and in the Highlands of Scotland, he had had his most extended experience in war. Although he had gained a reputation as a commander at Louisbourg such as would equip him for further appointments in the rank of brigadier or above, Canada had been the end of more than one hitherto fair military character. There was also the belief, justified over the years, that the further the distance from home, the more likely was a man to be forgotten, and Wolfe, having tasted success, knew his ambition to be as keen as ever. There would be no refusal on his part to serve, to whatever part of the world he was sent, but he had his inclinations.

Pitt had concluded that Amherst was the right man to command in chief the operations planned against Canada for 1759. He had proved his quality, and no better general was available. Whatever Wolfe's own appointment, assuming it to be across the Atlantic, he would once again be within the orbit of his late commander. Yet so little communication might be possible on active service that a principal subordinate could well find himself with complete responsibility for an independent enterprise.

Wolfe by Elizabeth, Duchess of Devonshire

In December 1758, not long after his return home, Wolfe was summoned to an interview by Lord Ligonier, the experienced and shrewd soldier who then held the position of commander-in-chief at home, and on whom Pitt relied for military advice. Ligonier, in the course of the discussion which resulted, disclosed Pitt's plan for Canada. 'We had some discourse,' wrote Wolfe to Amherst, 'concerning the navigation of the River St Lawrence, and upon the project of besieging

Quebec, and I found it was a settled plan to carry on two separate attacks, one on the side of Lake George and one up the River.' Wolfe had expressed his wish to go 'up the river,' but to be excused 'from taking the chief direction of such a weighty enterprise.' In spite of this uncharacteristically modest reservation, Pitt named him to the King for the river command. More surprisingly, the monarch agreed. It was very rare for him to give charge of any operation of scope to anyone but an officer of mature, sometimes of advanced years.

Wolfe continued to Amherst in an unusually sober mood, 'In short,' he wrote, 'they have put this heavy task on my shoulders, and I find nothing encouraging in the undertaking, but the warmest and most earnest desire to discharge so great a trust to your satisfaction as my General, and to his Majesty and the Publick. I shall spare no pains, and should be happy if the sacrifice of my own health and constitution, or even my life, could any how contribute to bring this bloody war to an honourable and speedy conclusion.'

If speech is given us to conceal our thoughts, it is equally true that the conventions of 18th century correspondence hid much that was meant to be read between the lines. Wolfe may have been something of a hypochondriac, but, if their letters are to be credited, so were many distinguished commanders of his time. Wolfe's health had long been precarious. He had had a hard life soldiering, and just before seeing Ligonier he had written to Captain Rickson 'I am in a very bad condition, both gravel and Rheumatism, but I would much rather die than decline any kind of service that offers.'

It is certain that no Colonel of just upon thirty-two, offered the prospect of trying to take Quebec, and with a commission as acting major general in his pocket, would ever have undertaken the assignment if his words to Amherst had in all respects been the literal truth. Such is not the spirit which animates successful operations. It should, however, be remarked that Wolfe anticipated closer liaison with Amherst in Canada than ever proved possible, and that he had not, when he wrote, more than a sketchy idea of what an enterprising admiral could do by way of approach to what was considered to be most formidable river obstacles.

Admiral Saunders

To his uncle, Major Walter Wolfe of Dublin, Wolfe opened his mind fully.

If the Marquis de Montcalm finds means to baffle our efforts another summer, he may be declared an able officer, or the Colony has resources that we know nothing of, or our Generals are worse than usual . . . I am to act a greater part in this business than I wished or desired. The backwardness of some of the older officers has in some measure forced the Government to come down so low. I shall do my best, and leave the rest to fortune, as perforce we must do when there are not the most commanding abilities . . . If I have health and constitution enough for the Campaign, I shall think of myself a lucky man; what happens afterwards is of no consequence.

II

The choice of naval commander fell on Charles Saunders. This left an aggrieved man in Sir Charles Hardy, who had done so well off Louisbourg, if not in later tasks. On board his flagship, which was at that time the *Hero*, Hardy poured out his woes to his friend Captain Augustus Hervey. He said that, as regards Quebec:

. . . he had been always made to believe by Lord Anson that he was to have gone . . . and that he was astonished when he found Mr. Saunders sent for to command that expedition on Mr. Boscawen's refusing it, that this was the more extraordinary and false in Lord Anson as Sir Charles, who had long been Governor of New York and well acquainted with all America, had shewn Lord Anson several papers and charts, etc., and that Saunders when named for the command wrote to Sir Charles Hardy for his advice and lights, declaring he knew nothing of the country, never having been therabouts. Sir Charles said he found there were those about Lord Anson who were jealous of Sir Charles's rank and getting too much credit by any command.

The admiral had a sympathetic listener. Hervey noted that the conversation 'only confirmed me in my opinion of Lord Anson's principles and abilities being of the very lowest class.' A man who believed that could believe anything, but Hervey had been a generous partisan of Byng. The judicial murder of that officer, which Anson had done nothing to prevent, was fresh in his mind, and his prejudice was understandable.

Saunders, who had been chosen for Quebec by Pitt and Anson, was not unlike his chief, whose pupil he was proud to be. He was the right age, being in his mid-forties – experienced enough not to be irresponsible, yet willing to take risks. Horace Walpole said of him that he was 'a pattern of the most sturdy bravery. No man said less or deserved more.' He had served with merit in Anson's famous circumnavigation of the previous decade, had been present at a major fleet action in the Atlantic under Hawke's command in 1747, and had been lucky both in a succession of good shore appointments such as Treasurer of

Greenwich Hospital and Comptroller of the Navy, which he owed to Anson, and in the matter of prize money at sea, which was partly due to his own exertions. Anson's officers all did well in later life, but during the course of the great voyage they had shown that they deserved to do so. Howe had been among them as a midshipman, though his ship was one of those which turned back before reaching the Pacific.

As his second-in-command, Saunders was to have Rear Admiral Philip Durell, who had been given his flag during the siege of Louisbourg. Durell's wife died while he was abroad, for he was among those left in North America, and news of her illness and death may have caused him to become less than alert and active at a time of crisis. But Wolfe had already formed a poor opinion of his capacity, and Durell's record suggests that such a view was not altogether ill-judged. Third in naval command would be Rear Admiral Charles Holmes, who had done well in recent North Sea operations, and would prove a tower of strength. Like Saunders, he was in his forties. He had had extended service already on the North American Station.

In Saunders's squadron were two men who were to have particularly notable careers. One was John Jervis, later Earl of

Captain Cook   *John Jervis, Lord St Vincent*

H.M.S. Sutherland, *Flagship of Rear Admiral Holmes*

St Vincent, who was first lieutenant of the flagship. The other, James Cook, sailing master of the *Pembroke*, was one day to become the world's greatest navigator.

Saunders's force was impressive. It included three ships of very large size: the *Neptune*, 90 guns, which was the Commander-in-Chief's flagship; the *Royal William*, 84 guns, and by far the oldest vessel present; and the *Princess Amelia*, 80 guns, which carried Durell's flag. Holmes flew his flag in the *Dublin* on board which vessel he had taken Amherst to America the previous year. Other ships with illustrious names or histories were the *Northumberland, Vanguard, Captain, Devonshire, Pembroke, Stirling Castle* and two smaller ships of the line, the *Sutherland*, 50 guns, and the *Centurion*, in which Anson had made his voyage of 1740–1744 when Saunders had served in her as a lieutenant. Frigates, fire-ships, bomb ketches and sloops were on an appropriate scale, and there were no less than 119 transports, ordnance vessels and victualling ships to swell a vast armada.

III

As military commander Wolfe was given three brigadiers, all of aristocratic birth. Two of them were of his own choice. The senior was the Honourable Robert Monckton, a son of Lord Galway, who was very little older than the general. After some earlier service in Flanders, Monckton had been sent to North America, where he had served six years, and done well. Wolfe does not seem to have known him intimately and his character is not easy to estimate. It was, no doubt, his experience that Wolfe looked to. One of the staff, at the close of the campaign, recorded the view that Monckton was 'of a dull capacity and may properly be called Fat Headed.' The brigadier's later career suggests that this view was misguided. Rodney, with whom Monckton co-operated at Martinique less than three years later, and with great success, found his opposite number of good understanding and equable temper.

The second brigadier, the Honourable George Townshend, was later to become a marquis, and a man of influence through his family connections. He could, however, be a difficult customer, one who had never been afraid of criticising authority. He had fallen out with the King's military son, the Duke of Cumberland, under whom he had served in Flanders, and it is doubtful if Wolfe would ever have considered him had it been left to his own initiative. He was three years older than the general, and pulled a number of strings to go on the expedition. Walpole reported him to be of a 'proud, sullen and contemptuous temper' and this was not far wrong. Wolfe accepted him with a show of grace, perhaps being flattered that so consequential a person, and one who could be so vociferous in Parliament, should have wished to go at all. He and Wolfe had both been associated with the 20th Foot, Townshend briefly, and they were at Dettingen together. Even then, when he was still in his teens, Townshend was a cool card. He was amazed at how the enemy were allowed to get away, unpursued. 'The King halted,' he remarked, 'and the scene of Action and military ardour was suddenly turned into a Court circle. His Majesty was congratulated by every military courtesan on horseback, on the glorious event!' A little earlier a drummer boy standing near Townshend had had his head struck off by a cannon ball, and this scattered his brains all round. An old soldier, thinking the young man might be dismayed at the incident, made some reassuring remark. Townshend replied: 'Oh, I'm not afraid, I'm only astonished that a fellow with such a quantity of brains should be here.'

James Murray, the third brigadier, was a dangerous man both on the field and off it. He was eaten up with ambition – like Wolfe, but with differences, since he was unscrupulous about how he attained his ends. He was a son of Lord Elibank, and his brother Alexander, who was well-known for his sympathies with the Pretender, was then in exile in France. Montcalm had a Jacobite in his army, the Chevalier Johnstone, and Murray could well have been on the same side. He grew to have a great regard for the Canadians, whom he was later to describe as 'perhaps the bravest and the best race upon the globe.'

An officer on Wolfe's staff left a series of valuable – unsigned notes about certain characters involved in the Quebec campaign.* Murray he described as 'the very Bellows of sedition; Envious, Ambitious, the very mention of another's merit canker'd him. Mr Wolfe's high reputation was more than Poison to him . . . Envy and Ambition are the only springs that work him.' If this seems severe, yet to the end of a long life Murray was to 'knock his obstinate Scotch head', as he put it, 'against the Admiration and Reverence of the English mob for Mr Wolfe's memory.' He was seven years older than his superior, and had seen varied service in Flanders, the West Indies, and elsewhere. After Rochefort he had given evidence in Mordaunt's favour at the official enquiry, which put him on the opposite side from Wolfe. But his conduct before Louisbourg was so meritorious that Wolfe wrote to Lord George Germain: 'Murray, my old antagonist, has acted with infinite spirit. The Publick is much indebted to him for advancing this Siege.' It was this side of Murray's character that led Wolfe to be glad of his services.

* They were acquired for his manuscript collection by Francis Dobbs (1750–1811), Irish poet and politician, and are now in the Public Record Office of Northern Ireland.

Isaac Barré   *Colonel Guy Carleton*

Two staff officers were able men destined for high rank in life.
Isaac Barré, the son of a French Protestant refugee from La
Rochelle who had settled in Dublin and done well there as a
merchant, was one. He was Adjutant General, and he later
showed a distinct gift as an orator. Of him, the note-taker wrote
that he was 'a worthy good man, with a great share of understanding and humour: brave, but still better qualified for the
Cabinet than the Field, and very proper as an Adjutant General.'
Barré once remarked of Pitt, to whose partiality he owed the
apoointment, 'No man ever entered his closet who did not feel
himself, if possible, braver on his return than when he went in.'
Guy Carleton, Quartermaster General, and later to become
Lord Dorchester, was the other. In a will made in Canada,
Wolfe left his papers to Carleton, who could thus have had
the opportunity, had his gifts lain that way, of being the
general's first biographer. The percipient note-taker observed
of Carleton that, though 'solid' he was 'not of quick capacity.'
Certainly he showed no inclination to memorialise Wolfe,
but his later life, the most important part of it spent in Canada,
proved him very able both as administrator and soldier.

Colonel Williamson, who commanded the artillery, was much loved, and took great care of his men. Lieutenant-Colonels Ralph Burton and William Howe were popular with Wolfe, and both men justified his faith in them. Burton might have been one of the brigadiers had he possessed the necessary seniority, and if Townshend had not stepped in. Captain Willaim Delaune was also smiled upon. He belonged to the 67th Foot, now Wolfe's own Regiment. Delaune and Howe would scale the Heights of Abraham together. Major Patrick MacKellar, the principal Engineer, was invaluable to Wolfe because he knew Quebec from a recent spell in the city as a prisoner of war. He had made notes and plans which, if not always exact and up-to-date, were better than anything else available.

Pitt had intended 12,000 soldiers for the St Lawrence, but sickness, desertion and other causes reduced this number considerably, so that Wolfe had about 8,500 men of his own Service under his immediate command. They were, however, excellent in quality, experienced in North American conditions, and they could be, and often were, supplemented by marines from the fleet. Apart from ten British line battalions, including Fraser's Highlanders, for whose officers Wolfe had much admiration, Wolfe was able to form another, drawn from the grenadier companies of three battalions left in garrison at Louisbourg, and usually called the Louisbourg Grenadiers. Wolfe knew the mettle of these men from the operations of the year before. Some units were below strength, but all were well trained.

There was no cavalry; on the other hand, three companies of the Royal Regiment of Artillery were given a powerful 'battering train' which again could be supplemented when necessary by guns from the ships. There were also six companies of American Rangers, four of them newly raised. These men were not militia recruited by Colonial legislation, but long service units raised under the Crown. During the course of the siege, 300 Colonial pioneers arrived as a reinforcement.

Wolfe sometimes referred to his 'small' army, but it was a good one, and it could draw on resources from the Navy which enlarged its strength. Neither Pitt nor Anson had stinted when it came to supporting Wolfe, and the fleet could be considered as one of the largest and best equipped ever given to the charge of a newly promoted Vice Admiral. Considering the calls made upon the Navy for other spheres of warlike activity, and the size of any possible opposition likely to be met with in North Atlantic waters, Saunders's margin of superiority was enormous. It indicated the importance which Pitt attached to Wolfe's expedition. This was emphasised in one of the secret instructions drafted by the Minister during the time Wolfe was at home.

Whereas the success of this expedition will very much depend upon an entire good understanding between our land and sea officers, we do strictly enjoin and require you, on your part, to maintain and cultivate such a good understanding and agreement and to order that the soldiers under your command shall man the ships when there shall be occasion for them, and when they can be spared from the land service. As the Commander-in-Chief of our Squadron is instructed, on his part, to entertain the same good understanding and agreement, and to order the sailors and marines under his command to assist our land forces and to man the batteries when there shall be occasion for them, and when they can be spared from the sea service; and in order to establish the strictest union that may be between you and the Commander-in-Chief of our ships, you are hereby required to communicate these instructions to him, as he is directed to communicate those he shall receive from us to you.

If this may have sounded like a counsel of perfection, the words were given far more emphasis, during the test of events, than had been accorded to similar admonitions in the past.

IV

Meanwhile the Governor General of New France, Pierre de Rigaud, Marquis de Vaudreuil, was preparing the Colony for the next phase of the war. Quebec was his home and his birth-place, for his father had become Governor General of New France in 1703 and held office twenty years, to general satisfaction. Pierre Vaudreuil, following a short stay in France, was made Governor General in 1755, when the frontiers were alight with the first clashes of the war. This in the upshot, was to ensure that his was the last appointment of its kind.

He had begun his career in the *troupes de marine* but had never seen combat service. What talent he had, and it was not excessive, was for administration. When Wolfe arrived before the town Vaudreuil was a man of just over sixty, eleven years of whose life had been spent as Governor of Louisiana, where he is remembered as *Le Grand Marquis*.

Pride in his country Vaudreuil undoubtedly possessed, and it would have been odd had this been otherwise. Naturally pompous, the trait had been encouraged by the positions he had held, first in Louisiana and then in Canada, where no one could dispute his eminence as the leader of society. He was affable, a characteristic which often goes with self-importance. He was also indulgent, not to say weak, towards those he liked, or he would never have tolerated the roguery of men like Bigot and Cadet, whom he actually praised in letters to France, to the

Marquis de Vaudreuil

sardonic amusement of some of the recipients. He was optimistic, often more so than the facts warranted, which could lead to neglect of necessary precautions; and he was suspicious of anyone with the slightest claim to dispute his decisions.

Francis Parkman, the American historian who gave years of his life to describing the Canada of Vaudreuil, said of the Governor General that he 'served the King and the Colony in some respects with ability, always with an unflagging zeal, and he loved the land of his birth with a jealous devotion that goes far towards redeeming his miserable defects.' If he had had more generosity in his nature he could, from his sad fate, have been an appealing person. As it was, he had few friends, and his warmest admirer was himself.

Affection has centred round Vaudreuil's military commander, Louis-Joseph, Marquis de Montcalm-Gozon, Seigneur de Saint-Véran. It is charged with that natural sympathy which goes out to the exile who longs for home. Montcalm's heart was

Marquis de Montcalm

with his wife and children, far away in his ancestral château of Candiac, in southern France. It was a house set in a countryside utterly different from the place where he had been sent to serve. 'I think I would give up all my honours to be back with you,' he wrote in his last letter to his wife, 'but the King must be obeyed. The moment I see you again will be the best of my life.'

In 1759 Montcalm was forty-seven, fifteen years older than Wolfe, and thirteen years younger than Vaudreuil. His life, like that of Wolfe, had been dedicated to his profession. His most noteworthy service had been during the War of the Austrian Succession. He had been wounded in the defence of Prague. At the battle of Piacenza, which had been disastrous for his side, he had been a regimental commander. His unit was practically wiped out, after he had twice rallied it, and he himself, disabled by sabre cuts, was taken prisoner. He was paroled, and later exchanged. Before the end of the war he had seen further active service as a brigadier, and was recognised as a gallant and efficient officer. His reward was appointment to the command of the *troupes de terre* and promotion to the rank of *maréchal de camp*, which corresponded to that of major-general in the British service.

In this role, one of his principal successes had been the taking of Fort William Henry, at the head of Lake George, during the course of the summer of 1757. The episode had been marked by the massacre of British prisoners by the Indians, which Montcalm had failed to prevent, though he deplored it. His great defensive victory at Ticonderoga the following year had added to his prestige with his regulars, though it had not improved his relationship with Vaudreuil, who liked to ascribe the credit for every success to his '*Canadiens*.'

Towards his officers Montcalm was cheerfully pessimistic, bantering, civilised. They were his own sort, and he knew how to treat them. However, his relationship with Vaudreuil was not so happy.

Although a clash of personalities must be accounted the chief reason, it was in some measure the complex organisation of the military forces of the country which widened the rift between Vaudreuil and Montcalm. It began to appear not long after the arrival of Montcalm from France in 1756. As Governor General,

Soldier of Le Régiment de la Reine, 1759

Quebec before the siege

Vaudreuil considered himself to be in supreme and not merely in nominal charge of all the Canadian armed forces, not excluding the disposition of the regular troops. Had the two men been friends, the mischief which so often attends divided command would have been reduced, if not eliminated: as it was, it grew worse.

The Lieutenant of New France was François Bigot. He had piled up an immense fortune, which he was adding to yearly, and his minions followed his lead. Corruption was common in that age, but when the whole truth came out, it shocked France. Bigot's principal abbettor was Joseph Cadet, who became *munitionnaire general*, and his exactions were such that after the end of the war, judges in Paris ordered him to make good six million *livres*.

Canada was a land of small landlords and farmers, peasants, priests and *coureurs de bois* who were engaged in the fur trade. Montreal and Quebec were the only towns large enough to attract professional men and merchants, and the permanent population of Quebec, which has been variously estimated, was not more than 7,000. Every able-bodied man was called upon to serve in arms, and the defences of the country had recently been strengthened by a body of regulars from France who were known as *troupes de terre*. Besides these highly trained soldiers were the *troupes de la marine*. These were regulars locally raised, and so called not from any connection with the navy but because of the Minister in France who looked after the Colonies. Finally there was the citizen force, the militia, numbering about 15,000. Every parish had its company, and in times of crisis everyone, in theory, would be in arms, though defections were common, particularly when crops needed attention. There were also Indian 'allies', whose allegiance varied with whichever side was on top. Montcalm called them *ces villains messieurs*. Wolfe was less polite. He thought of them as a 'dastardly set of bloody rascals', which from his own point of view was an exact description.

After the siege of Louisbourg, when there were still some fears for Quebec that summer on the part of the French, Montcalm sent a young officer to Versailles to explain the difficulties facing the authorities in New France, and to plead its cause at the Court of Louis XV. The man chosen was Louis-Antoine de Bougainville. He was a messenger equally acceptable to Vaudreuil, whose daughter looked upon him with particular favour.

Bougainville was not yet thirty. As he was to show accomplishments in many sides of life, and as he lived to be valued by Napoleon I in a very different era, he has claim to be one of the most interesting figures, as well as the most civilised, on either side in the campaign which was to be the natural sequence of the events of 1758. Like a less estimable character in Dryden's *Absalom and Achitophel* he was –

> A man so various that he seemed to be,
> Not one, but all mankind's epitome.

A Parisian, Bougainville had originally trained for the law. Even before taking up what was to prove to be only a brief career in the army, he had shown talent in diplomacy, and he had written a treatise on integral calculus which had won him election in London to the Fellowship of the Royal Society and brought him many English friends. After his service in Canada he transferred to the Navy. He commanded a ship of the line under de Grasse in the battle of the Chesapeake, where French sea power helped to ensure the successful revolt of the American Colonies against Great Britain, and later at the Saints Passage, off Dominica, when Rodney achieved a victory by breaking the French line. Somewhat earlier, concurrently with the first of Cook's three voyages, Bougainville had made a circumnavigation, of which he wrote a valuable account. Today he is perhaps best remembered for having introduced an increasingly popular semi-tropical plant, the *Bougainvillea*, to other parts of the world.

Bougainville's ship evaded Durell's blockading squadron at Louisbourg and duly reached France, to find a country economically strained, though with many war plans. One of the more important was still secret. It was a project for the invasion of Britain, a temptation which was to recur over and over again in France and Spain, always to come to nothing.

Madame de Pompadour

It was as a diplomat that Montcalm called upon Bougainville's services, and a more persuasive envoy could not have been chosen. Among other things he managed to gain the ear of Madame de Pompadour, who at that time ruled France through the attention which Louis XV paid to her by night and day.

However, there was not much interest to spare at Versailles for remote Canada. This was nothing new, and when Bougainville spoke with the Minister responsible for the Colonies he was met with the words: 'Monsieur, when the house is on fire, one doesn't bother about the stables.' Bougainville's reply is well-known. 'At least,' he said, 'no one will say that you talk like a horse!'

Montcalm appreciated the difficulties of sending powerful reinforcements to Canada in the face of British naval strength, and did not hope for them. 'It is evident' noted his emissary, 'that the Government must for the present treat Canada like a sick man, to be kept alive with cordials. If we can survive this year's crisis we are justified in hoping the country will be saved for good.' What Montcalm proposed, strategically, was a

Louis XV

Comte de Bougainville

diversion against Virginia and the Carolinas. He recommended that direct aid should consist of drafts to fill gaps in his regular battalions, together with a number of engineers and artillerymen who were badly needed. He also asked for field guns and small arms, ammunition, trade goods for the Indians and, most vital of all, foodstuffs to help make good the deficiencies of a poor harvest. As this was modest enough, especially in terms of manpower, the request was looked on favourably.

Montcalm also put forward a scheme – neat and logical, such as might appeal to the French mind – for better use of Canadian resources. He recommended a census dividing man into three classes, good, moderate and bad, and suggested that all the good men should serve throughout the next campaign. These would in turn be divided into three groups, one being drafted into the regular French battalions, one into units of colonial regulars, while a third would serve separately as militia. This was approved.

Another scheme put forward indicates how slender a hope Montcalm held out for a successful defence of Canada. He proposed that if a capitulation became inevitable, the regular troops, together with the best of the colonials, should withdraw down the Mississippi to Louisiana. Bougainville reported that this notion was regarded by the Court with surprise, and it was promptly turned down.

V

Meanwhile Saunders sailed from Spithead on 17 February 1759 with Wolfe on board the *Neptune*. With them went the ships-of-the-line *Royal William, Dublin, Shrewsbury, Warspite, Orford, Alcide* and *Stirling Castle*. There was a frigate, the *Lizard*, the *Scorpion*, sloop of war, three fire-ships, the *Cormorant, Strombolo* and *Vesuvius*, and the bomb-vessels, *Baltimore, Pelican* and *Racehorse*. A smaller detachment under Holmes had sailed a few days earlier.

While off the coast of Spain, orders reached the Admiral to detach two ships to reinforce Boscawen in the Mediterranean. One of those named was the *Stirling Castle*, 60 guns, but Saunders, knowing the value that smaller ships of the line were likely to have in the confined waters of the St Lawrence, sent the larger *Warspite* instead.

Saunders had much to occupy him at sea, and it was not in Wolfe's nature to be idle. On 6 March, from mid-Atlantic, he wrote to Amherst complaining of the size of his force and suggesting that it would have been better if Amherst himself, with fifteen or more battalions, had been sent up the St Lawrence. He then went on:

If, by accident in the River, by the Enemy's resistance, by sickness, or slaughter in the Army, or from any other cause, we find that Quebec is not likely to fall into our hands (persevering however to the last moment), I propose to set the Town on fire with Shells, to destroy the Harvest, Houses and Cattle both above and below, to send off as many Canadians as possible to Europe, & to leave famine and desolation behind me; *belle resolution et très chréstienne!* but we must teach these Scoundrels to make war in a more gentleman-like manner.

This was not a pretty programme, but Wolfe had no illusions about the nature of warfare, or of the treatment compatriots had suffered at enemy hands in recent engagements. The aftermath of Fort William Henry was fresh in his mind.

Wolfe looked after his soldiers vigilantly, but as he had stated often, particularly after Rochefort, he would sacrifice them without hesitation if he thought this could be justified. His men were expendable – so was he. The troops knew this, and they knew him to be personally fearless in action. The same anonymous staff officer at Quebec who made such damaging remarks about army and navy personalities alike, wrote that Wolfe 'work'd up Courage to such a pitch in his little army that it became necessary often to desire the Soldiers not to expose themselves without a necessity for it.'

Wolfe and the Admiral remained on cordial terms on the voyage, but, during their weeks in immediate contact, Saunders was cautious. It was his way, but he had special reasons for not giving Wolfe any close idea of his tactical plans. He suspected the general of impetuosity, in which he was quite right. Also, he did not know precisely what he could do until he was well up the river. Wolfe, however, had a shrewd notion of the sort of support he expected from Saunders. As early as 19 May he wrote to his uncle Walter, who had replaced his father as his principal family confidant:

It is the business of our naval force to be masters of the River, both above and below the Town. If I find the Enemy is strong, audacious and well commanded, I shall proceed with the utmost caution and circumspection, giving Mr. Amherst time to use his superiority. If they are timid, weak and ignorant, we shall push them with more vivacity, that we may be able before the summer is gone to assist the Commander-in-Chief. I reckon we shall have a smart action at the passage of the river St. Charles, unless we can steal a detachment up the river St. Lawrence, and land them three, four, five miles or more above the Town, and get time to entrench so strongly that they won't care to attack.

This was all speculation. What was immediate fact was the series of shocks which occurred before ever he sent off his letter. The winter in Canada had been one of the severest within memory, and the ice in the Gulf of St Lawrence had taken far longer than usual to break up. Moreover, the *Namur* had had a difficult passage. April 20th had been the day arranged for the concentration of all the forces at Louisbourg, for Pitt was determined that no time whatever should be lost, as it had been the previous year. Yet it was not until the very end of the month that Saunders sighted Cape Breton. Even then it was impossible to approach the coast. For over a week the Admiral persisted in trying to find a way through, and then bore away for Halifax. There, to his amazement and dismay, he found Durell still at anchor.

It is difficult to imagine contemporaries of the calibre of Richard Howe or Sir Charles Hardy acting, or rather, failing to act, like Durell, especially after the warnings and reminders he had had of the importance of preventing any French ships from entering the St Lawrence. Durell's place, however, chilling it might be, was waiting and patrolling at the edge of the ice, with the strongest force he could muster. He was then likely to intercept, for no French ship could go where he could not.

Saunders discovered that Durell's squadron had been ready for sea for over a month, and that his subordinate had been waiting until he had reports that the ice would allow him to move freely in the Gulf. 'Had we but sailed,' wrote one of Durell's officers in exasperation to Governor Lawrence at Halifax, 'at the time you so earnestly wished, we had most certainly intercepted the French, as they were not more than ten days ahead of us.' To stay at Halifax until he knew for certain that the area of the St Lawrence was navigable was to make it all too probable that the vessels expected so eagerly from France would get ahead of him.

That is exactly what happened.

VI

The ships included one which carried Bougainville, though he
had to wait eighteen days for a reasonably ice-free passage. He
had embarked at Bordeaux, given the British cruisers the slip,
and reached Quebec on 10 May 1759, without having sighted
a single hostile unit. Seldom can an officer have brought news of
more importance. For just as he left France, Bougainville had
been given a copy of a letter from Amherst to the Government
in London disclosing the whole outline of the British campaign
plans, including information of the formidable preparations
which were being made for an attack up the St Lawrence. This
had been intercepted on its way across the Atlantic.

At no time was security good during the subsequent Quebec
campaign, for there was far too much interchange between the
opposing forces by means of prisoners and deserters. The tone
was set at the beginning, the French knowing everything with
which they were likely to be faced.

Wolfe's staff officer's notes were particularly severe at this
time, and with reason. The writer had no words harsh enough
for Durell and his captains. 'They begin to see themselves in a
devilish scrape,' he wrote, 'and that they should be called to
account for not being in the Chops of the River early enough to
prevent supplies going to Quebec . . . All mankind joined in an
opinion that nothing could be more scandalous than their
proceedings, and all the Bellowing of the Troops at Halifax
could not persuade them to leave the harbour for fear of ice.
Canada would certainly have been an easy conquest had the
Squadron gone early into the River.'

Bougainville did not get in alone. Two other frigates as well
as his own, and nearly a score of supply ships, followed up.
Although the reinforcement in men was modest – 400 replace-
ments, 40 gunners and a few engineers, besides some material –
when a country is reduced to the state in which New France
found herself during the early months of 1759, a little could
be made to go a long way.

When Bougainville reached Quebec, relations between
Montcalm and Vaudreuil, the Governor-General of Canada,
were as bad as anything which could possibly have developed

between Wolfe and his subordinates, and they were now to deteriorate still further. Vaudreuil was instructed to defer to Montcalm in military matters, but the wording of the order is in odd contrast to the clarion call Pitt addressed to Wolfe regarding co-operation with Saunders. 'His Majesty's intention,' so the order ran, 'is that M. le Marquis de Montcalm shall not only be consulted on all operations, but also on all areas of administration relating to the defence and preservation of the Colony: you will ask his advice, communicating to him the letters I shall write to you on all these subjects.'

Montcalm was given the rank of Lieutenant-General in recognition of his success against Abercromby. Vaudreuil – certainly with the concurrence of Bougainville, who could see only too well how much depended on smoother relationships between the two men, and the effect of a promotion for Montcalm without a sweetener to the Governor General – was given the Grand Cross of the Order of St. Louis. And, since in the 18th century bearers of good things, naval or military, were accustomed to awards, sometimes out of proportion to the news announced, which in this case was merely full details of Ticonderoga, Bougainville received the rank of colonel, and the Cross of the same Order which would be worn by Vaudreuil.

The general instructions for Canada were that Vaudreuil and Montcalm should stand on the defensive and do their utmost to hold at least a part of the Colony until fresh orders could be sent out in 1760. Immediate help would consist of four royal ships carrying munitions and trade goods. Encouragement would also be given to private suppliers to forward provisions. That was all.

VII

Once jolted out of his inertia Durell was, if anything, better than his orders, though by this time the mischief had been done. Pushing on, he anchored off Ile aux Coudres on 28 May, but found the place deserted. Next day, Carleton landed a few men to reconnoitre. When word of this reached Quebec, a party of Canadians and Indians was sent off to try to take a prisoner, for the sake of information.

The foray came to little, doubtless because of the majestic presence of Durell's flag-ship, the *Princess Amelia*, but some returning islanders, proceeding by stealth, picked up three midshipmen who were sky-larking about the island on stray horses. They were ambushed and taken off to Quebec – the whole incident could well come out of a novel by Captain Marryat. Actually the youngsters were there for the purpose of 'making Signals on seeing any Ships or Vessels coming up, or going down the River.' Durell issued orders next day for-bidding soldiers or sailors to 'harrass' horses when ashore. Two of the midshipmen had been riding on the same beast. It was more fun than tamely watching out for French ships.

Naval officers say that when an admiral of dynamic leader-ship in war hoists his flag, the effect seems to be felt right down to the keels of the ships. It was so with the army assembled at Louisbourg when at last, in mid-May, it came face to face with Wolfe. Here was a general that some of the men knew already, and whatever divergent opinions there may have been about him, there was agreement on one thing, that he had a 'peculiar turn for War.' He was young, and so were they, so it was unlikely they would dither about. 'Young troops must be encouraged,' he wrote, and how right he was. 'What appears hazardous sometimes,' he added 'is usually not so to people who know the country.' It was early summer, and there was a feeling that by autumn or winter many could be home again, trailing if not clouds of glory, then at least a wisp or two.

Wolfe's appearance in itself was striking. He described him-self as having a 'long, bony figure' and this is borne out by contemporary drawings, which also emphasise his neatness of dress: a smart officer, who would expect the same in his men; smart, but not showy. He was indeed very thin. Some years earlier he had written from Scotland: 'if I say I am thinner, you will imagine me a shadow or skeleton in motion. In short I am everything but what the surgeons call a subject for anatomy. As far as muscles, bones and the larger vessels conserve their purpose, they have a clear view of them in me, distinct from fat or fleshy impediment.' It is not given to many to see them-selves so objectively.

Brigadier Townshend, who was a gifted amateur artist,

drew Wolfe, head and shoulders, and coloured the portrait, which he gave to Isaac Barré, who valued it all his life. When he came upon it, Robert Wright, Wolfe's early biographer, wrote on the top: 'Though slight, this is the most convincing portrait of Wolfe I have ever seen.' It still is, for Townshend managed to convey the living breath of that eager spirit, as well as the red hair, blue eyes, rather thin lips, and the neat queue, which other portraits bear out less vividly. Townshend's version is nearly full face, but a profile would have reinforced the impression of vitality. Wolfe had a large and arrow-like nose, and a receding chin which is so often, and so often erroneously with weakness of character. There was no weakness here, at least as regards essentials, and what few have remarked is the resemblance between Wolfe's profile and that of the younger Pitt, the second son of the great War Minister, who happened to be born the year that Wolfe died.

Wolfe looked at his men, and reported to Amherst – 'I believe they feel stout.' They had need to be, for there were not as many as had been hoped. When some officers, knowing Wolfe's reputation, guarded themselves against rebuke by saying that their men did not know yet some new exercises that had recently been prescribed, they had a sharp reply. 'New exercises – new fiddlesticks,' said Wolfe, 'if they are otherwise well disciplined and will fight, that's all I shall require of them.'

Wolfe knew most of the Line regiments already, the 15th, 28th, 35th, 43rd, 47th, 48th, 58th and the Royal Americans. Then there were the Highlanders, the 78th. Wolfe was as well acquainted with Highlanders as any officer then serving, so much of his time had been spent in their country both campaigning and on garrison duty. But the 78th had a very particular distinction. They were, mainly, Frasers.

Simon Fraser, twelfth baron Lovat, had taken part in the risings of 1715 and 1745 which had been intended to restore the Stuarts. In the '15 he had been on the Government side but in the '45, having been promised a dukedom by the Pretender, he supported Prince Charles Edward. Later, he was caught, tried and beheaded.

The old rebel's eldest son, the Master of Lovat, also took part in the '45 but was pardoned. In 1756/7 he returned to his

Men of the Lancashire Militia

father's estates, where in a few weeks he raised a battalion of over 1,400 men for service with the royal forces. These men he took to America, where they invariably fought with distinction. At least two other Simon Frasers had commissions in the 78th who due course rose, like their colonel, to the rank of brigadier or above.

Wolfe felt least sure about the detachments of American Rangers which were part of his army, and these troops, in the main, were not drawn from the better type of citizen. Their rank even included a few Indians. It was noted that there had been no mad rush in the Colonies to join the colours, in spite of the fact that it was the Americans who had most to gain from the campaign. But on the whole the men promised well. 'Our troops are good and very well disposed,' the general reported. 'If valour can make amends for want of numbers, we shall probably succeed.'

In the messes, where naval and military officers lived as far as possible together, there was a spirit of optimism. 'British colours on every French fort, port and garrison in America' – such was the toast. Wolfe's orders had a sense of purpose, and were expressed in manly style. Some of them cause audible relief: for instance, sensible changes were made in the often ridiculous uniforms in which soldiers were expected to fight. The cut of the coat for the companies of Light Infantry, the scouting troops, was made freer. Lace was removed from the cuffs. Additional pockets for ball and flints for the muskets were to be sewn on. Knapsacks were to be carried higher and fastened with 'a scrap of web over the shoulders, as the Indians carry their packs.' That was exactly the sort of improvement, the result of watching the enemy, that Colonel Lord Howe had suggested before his untimely death. Cartridge boxes hung under the left arm, powder horns under the right. Bayonet and tomahawk hung from the belt. Although the grenadier companies retained their mitre-like head gear,★ so imposing on a tall man since it increased his height, but sometimes ludicrous on a small one, the Light Infantryman's hat was converted into a cap 'with as much black cloth added as will come under his chin, and keep him warm when he lies down.' All this, the soldiers knew, was the result of careful thought. It was what was rarely given to their needs.

The Hanoverian kings liked to dress their men on Prussian models, without any consideration for comfort or utility. Ruffles, gaiters, pipe-clayed belts and so on made the men look like toy soldiers. One of the more literate men recorded that his uniform was made 'so tight and braced up so firm that we almost stood like automata of wood, mechanically arranged for some exhibition on a large scale. To stoop was more than our

---

★ This bore the legend *Nec aspera terrent*, which could be rendered: 'Difficulties do not dismay us.'

Cap of the 43rd Regiment

small clothes were worth, buttons flying, knees bursting, back
parts rending, and the long heavy groan when we stood up, just
like an old gouty corpulent man stooping to lift his fallen
crutch!' Finally, there was the powdered and plaited hair which
lasted into the 19th century. 'It was no uncommon circumstance,' wrote the same sufferer, 'when on the guard-bench and
asleep, to have rats and mice scrambling about our heads, eating
the filthy stuff with which our hair was bedaubed.' It is small
wonder that the army was unpopular, or that Encyclopaedias
sometimes differentiated between 'Intelligence, General' and
'Intelligence, Military.'

The burden of gaudy uniform was not the first or last of a soldier's trials. There was his equipment or baggage, what the Romans so aptly called *impedimenta*. On active service, a private carried a total weight of about 50 lbs. Some of this lumber was vital, some useful, and much ridiculous. Essential was the musket, nick-named, and with affection, Brown Bess. It weighed 10 lb. 12 oz. and had a bayonet weighing just over a pound. It was to show itself to be one of the heroes of Wolfe's campaign. The barrel was nearly four foot long and the bore was .75 of an inch. The bore of the ball was appreciably smaller, to facilitate ease of loading. This ball was contained in a paper cartridge. When some powder had been shaken into the priming pan and the remainder, plus the ball itself, put down the barrel, the cartridge acted as a wad. The flint-lock was stamped Tower, indicating the place of origin, and it also bore the Crown and Royal Cipher.

Brown Bess had first been brought into service in about 1720, and it was known, more officially, as the Long Land musket. It was standard equipment all through the Seven Years War except in some Highland units which had carbines, and it was not superseded for some ten years after its use at Quebec, when a version with a slightly shorter barrel became standard. The French in Canada thought Brown Bess much superior to their own weapon, but the superiority came from better training, and from the smaller ball used by the British. The idea of an officer such as Wolfe, who excelled at tactical drill, was to enable troops to fire about three well directed volleys per minute at as close a range as possible, so that every ball had a chance to hit.

Besides his musket, a private soldier was supposed to have a week's iron rations with him and a cooking pot, three shirts, two white stocks, one black stock, three pairs of oiled linen

Brown Bess muskets

stockings for marching – oiled to avoid sores, and to keep off some of the effects of the weather – one pair of spatterdashes (elegant leg coverings rising to the knee and buttoned at the side), two pairs of black linen gaiters and one pair of woollen gaiters, one pair of drawers, which may seem spartan, but then they did not show, a cap, cockade, cloak, knapsack, haversack, one pair of shoe buckles, one pair of garter buckles, two pairs of shoes, 24 rounds of ball cartridge in a cartouche which was – hopefully – fairly waterproof, two flints, and a ramrod. It was an Irishman, Shaw, who wrote, in *The Devil's Discipline*, that 'the British soldier can stand up to anything except the British War Office.' Perhaps the reason was that, by and large, his adversaries in the field were just as fantastically burdened. They could scarcely be more so. If the idea had been to handicap troops before battle, it was brilliantly carried out.

There was indeed a lot to be learnt from the Canadiens and the Indians, in respect of equipment as well as in guerilla warfare, but as Wolfe hoped to defeat Montcalm in formal battle, Continental style, the regulars could not be allowed too much relaxation of method and training.

It was while he was still at Louisbourg that Wolfe had news of the death of his father. A full-length sketch by an ADC, Captain Harvey Smith, shows the general wearing a black arm-band. It was an odd circumstance that he should have had this particular news when conducting a Combined Operation, for the very first military arrangement of his life was for him to have accompanied his father in 1740 to Cartagena, an affair which had been in the riper tradition of inter-Service bungles. Luckily illness, not his tender years, kept him at home.

The troops were bound to spend a lot of time on board ship, in crowded conditions and with little to do. An Order, which was dated early in May, insisted that officers should give special attention to the health of their men. 'Guards must mount in every ship,' he said, 'to keep strict order and prevent fire.' When the weather allowed, men should be in the open air as much as possible, and they were to eat on deck. Finally: 'cleanliness in the berths and bedding, and as much exercise as the situation permits, are the best preservatives of health.'

Early in June, the regiments were embarked, and after the

Wolfe sketched by Hervey Smyth

usual delays due to fog and adverse winds, they were off to the St Lawrence, more than three months after Wolfe had left Spithead, and with three or at best four months campaigning weather left. How right was Pitt to insist on watching the calendar not with the eye of hope but with the wisdom of experience.

Even after the expedition had sailed on the last part of their journey, Saunders was still non-commital. Wolfe wrote, as they approached the St Lawrence, 'The Admiral is a zealous brave officer. I don't know exactly the disposition he intends to make . . . but I conclude he will send four or five of his smallest ships

Grenadiers of the 47th and 48th Regiments of Foot

of the line to assist us at Quebec, and remain with the rest at anchor below the Isle of Coudres, ready to fight whatever Fleet the enemy may send to disturb us.'

VIII

No one had yet succeeded in taking a hostile fleet of any size any distance up the St Lawrence. This was because of the supposedly difficult navigation, due to tides – with a rise and fall of nineteen feet near Quebec – currents, eddies, and uncharted rocks.

In 1711, within the memory of older people, an expedition had come to grief, far down the river. The joint commanders had been Rear Admiral Sir Hovenden Walker and Brigadier John Hill, the brother of Abigail Masham, favourite of Queen Anne. They had got no nearer to Quebec than 300 miles and were in the neighbourhood of Egg Island, on the north shore west of Anticosti when they were overtaken by a storm which wrecked several ships and cost many lives. The operations were abandoned forthwith. The citizens of Quebec, who had named their church Notre Dame de la Victoire, in the Lower Town, in celebration of the repulse of Sir William Phips by Frontenac twenty-one years earlier, promptly altered Victoire into the plural. Phips had been defeated ashore. Walker and Hill had been foiled by natural forces.

Quebec relied on some such divine help in 1759. The churches and convents echoed with prayers on the subjects as soon as it was known that the British were in the river, but Saunders was of different stuff from Walker, and so were his captains. Early on, Durell seemed to have achieved something at last when he lured a number of local pilots aboard his ships by hoisting false colours, but it is doubtful if they would ever have been of much use, for they made difficulties where there were none. No doubt they regarded this as part of their duty to their country: at any rate many of them were sure that, even if Saunders with his ships did get up the river, they would never get down again.

They were to be proved wrong, and this was due to the collaboration of three of the many remarkable men who were with the expedition. Two of them, Samuel Jan Holland, and

Joseph Frederick Wallet Des Barres, were military: the third
was James Cook.

Whatever Admiral Durell's way of employing the very
severe winter at Halifax may have been, Cook, then serving as
sailing master of the *Pembroke*, gave his time to the study of
navigation, his life-work. He was fortunate in that John Simcoe,
the captain of his ship, shared all his zeal for knowledge. At
this time, and possibly for some decades to come, the military
surveyors were to have the advantage, technically, of their
naval counterparts. Cook had the priceless chance of instruction
from Holland and Des Barres, two of the best.

Holland had been born, as his name suggests, in the Low
Countries, and he had served with the Dutch army until 1755.
Then he had transferred to British service and had been sent to
North America, where he was to spend the most fruitful years
of a long life.

Des Barres could well have been on the French side, for his
family were Huguenots. They had left France as the result of the
Revocation of the Edict of Nantes, which had tolerated
Protestants, by Louis XIV. This was a political decision which
resulted in fearful persecution, and in the exodus from the
dominions of the King of France of some of the most enlightened
characters, to the lasting benefit of other countries, not least
Great Britain.

Des Barres had been given a commission in the Royal
American Regiment in 1756, and had later raised a corps of field
artillery. He had also served with distinction against the Indians,
some of whom he had won over to the British cause. He had
attracted Wolfe's notice during the siege of Louisbourg. Like
Holland, he spent much of the rest of his life in North America,
and as he lived to be a hundred and two, surviving until 1824,
he is likely to have been the last soldier to have been able to
recollect details of the campaign of 1759.

It is disputed from which of these two exceptional and gifted
men Cook learnt most. The three were much of an age – in their
thirties, with hard practical experience and close acquaintance
with responsibility. Each of them was preparing as best he could
for those higher flights of command to which, in the course of
time, each would be called. The immediate gain was that their

combined resources resulted in a splendid series of surveys of the St Lawrence which were published, on a scale of an inch to a mile, as early as 1760.

Captain John Simcoe had died before Wolfe's expedition was in train, and the command of the *Pembroke* developed upon Captain John Wheelock, but Holland, writing many years later to Simcoe's son, who had by then become Lieutenant-Governor of Upper Canada, gives a valuable glimpse of Cook and his captain at work in the winter months before Quebec.

During our stay in Halifax, [so runs his account] whenever I could get a moment of time from my duty, I was on board the *Pembroke* where the great cabin, dedicated to scientific purpose and mostly taken up with a drawing table, furnished no room for idlers. Under Capt. Simcoe's eye, Mr. Cook and myself compiled materials for a chart of the Gulf and River St. Lawrence, which plan at Capt. Simcoe's decease was dedicated to Sir Charles Saunders; with no other alterations than what Mr. Cook and I made coming up the river.

It was not to be doubted that, with such abilities at their command, Wolfe and Saunders could rely on the accuracy of their map-makers. In fact, no expedition of the 18th century is better documented in this respect.

On 3 June Durell ordered Captain William Gordon of the *Devonshire* to take under his charge the *Centurian, Pembroke* and *Squirrel*, escorting three transports, and to go with them as far up the river as the Isle of Orleans, or as much higher as he found practicable. He was to destroy fire rafts which had been reported as being made ready by the French, and to collect information. Colonel Carleton went with him.

Owing to adverse winds, Gordon could not get away from Coudres until five days later, which was a delay, typical of the weather, such as not the most eager officer could prevent, but by the afternoon of 8 June Gordon was at the foot of the famous Traverse Channel. This the French counted upon as the principal difficulty facing the besiegers as they neared Quebec.

Early on 9 June the *Devonshire* signalled for 'all boats man'd and arm'd in order to go and sound the Channel of the Traverse.' The work continued next day, and on the 11th James Cook of the *Pembroke* 'returned satisfied with being acquainted with ye

Channel.' If Cook said that, any seaman would have known things would be well.

By far the best account of the actual navigation came from Captain John Knox, of the 43rd Foot, who was on board one of the later transports, the *Goodwill*. His narrative states what happened in a ship which, benefitting by the careful work of those that which had gone before, made the passage later in the month, when the feat had become commonplace in the advanced squadron.

At 3 p.m. on 25 June a French pilot was put on board each transport, and the man who fell to the *Goodwill's* lot gasconaded at a most extravagant rate, and gave us to understand it was much against his inclination that he was to become an English pilot.

The poor fellow assumed great latitude in his conversation, said he made no doubt that some of the fleet would return to England, but that they should have a dismal tale to carry with them; for

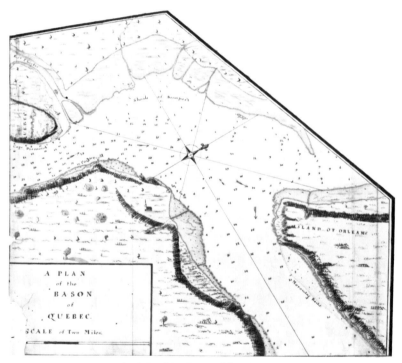

Detail of Cook's chart of the St Lawrence

Canada should be the grave of the whole Army, and he expected in a short time, to see the walls of Quebec ornamented with English scalps. Had it not been in obedience to the Admiral, who gave orders that he should not be ill used, he would certainly have been thrown overboard.

At 4 p.m. we passed the Travers, which is reputed a place of the greatest difficulty and danger between the entrance of the St. Lawrence and Quebec: it lies between Cape Tourmente (a remarkably high, black-looking promontory) and the east end of Orleans on the starboard side and the Isle de Madame on the larboard. Off Orleans we met some of our ships of war at anchor. As soon as the pilot came on board today, he gave his directions for the working of the ship, but the Master would not permit him to speak; he fixed his Mate at the helm, charged him not to take orders from any person except himself, and going forward with his trumpet to the forecastle, gave the necessary instructions.

All that could be said by the Commanding Officer and the other gentleman on board was to no purpose; the pilot declared we should be lost, for that no French ship ever presumed to pass there without a pilot. 'Ay, ay, my dear,' replied our son of Neptune, 'but d—— me, I'll convince you that an Englishman shall go where a Frenchman dare not show his nose!'

The *Richmond* frigate being close astern of us, the Commanding Officer called out to the Captain, and told him our case; he inquired who the Master was, and was answered from the forecastle by the man himself, who told him he was old Killick, and that was enough.

I went forward with this experienced mariner, who pointed out the Channel to me as we passed, showing me by the ripple and colour of the water, where there was any danger; and distinguishing the places where there were ledges of rock (to me invisible) from banks of sand, mud or gravel. He gave his orders with great unconcern, joked with the sounding-boats who lay off each side with different-coloured flags for our guidance; and when any of them called to him, and pointed to the deepest water, he answered, 'Ay, ay, my dear, chalk it down – a d—— dangerous navigation, eh? If you don't make a sputter about it, you'll get no credit for it in England, etc.'

After we had cleared that remarkable place, where the Channel forms a complete zig-zag, the Master called to his Mate to give the helm to somebody else, saying 'D—— me if there are not a thousand places in the Thames fifty times more hazardous than this; I am ashamed that Englishmen should make such a rout about it.' The Frenchman asked me if the Captain had not been here before. I assured him in the negative, upon which he viewed him with great attention, lifting, at the same time, his eyes and hands to heaven with astonishment and fervency.

The very day of these occurrences, Montcalm noted in a letter to one of his brigadiers that even the French themselves would not have a good chart of the river before the following year, and he recorded his view that 'our best seamen or pilots seem to me either liars or ignoramuses.'

Wolfe himself was in the frigate *Richmond*, immediately behind the *Goodwill*. He was anxious to see the size of his task as soon as possible and the captain had orders to take the general wherever he wished. The same day of the incident noted by Knox, Saunders himself reached Coudres and transferred his flag to the *Stirling Castle*. He then, in his turn, passed up the river. Durrell, with the larger ships, was left on guard downstream. This was to ensure that no French force would menace the rear – at least without warning. Before the end of July Durell had moved up very near Quebec. Even the great *Neptune* was there by 4 August.

Major Mackellar had recommended the Isle of Orleans as the best place for an initial landing. The idea was accepted. As Wolfe and his engineer surveyed the scene from the most westerly point of the island, to which they pushed through the woods, they had an awe-inspiring prospect in their telescopes as they focussed on Quebec. But they also took in the nature of the military problem. It was not a light one. The enemy had been given time, and had not wasted it.

PART THREE

THE
FIRST ATTEMPT

Quebec · Combined Services
Manoeuvering · Attack · Pause
Wolfe's Fever

THE
FIRST ATTEMPT

I

A FIRST sight of Quebec is unforgettable. The city, with its Upper and Lower Town, built on a commanding rock on the north bank of the St Lawrence, is nearly 700 miles from the open Atlantic, yet it is the first great centre up the river. Everything about it, including the wooded contours of the surrounding country, is on a scale of splendour. There, the St Lawrence, which Jacques Cartier originally named the River of Canada, widens suddenly into a huge basin. The Upper Town, where once stood the residence of the French Governor, is 200 feet above the water. The highest point of the city peninsula, nearly 350 feet, is further west, at Cape Diamond, the site of the modern Citadel.

In Wolfe's time the French had protected the harbour, on the north side of the city, with a boom, and a floating battery of twelve guns, the harbour itself being at the confluence of the river St Charles with the main stream. Across the St Charles was a pontoon bridge so that troops could move quickly from east to west of the city. Six miles to the north east the small Montmorency empties its waters into the St Lawrence over a fall, more than a hundred feet higher than Niagara. On the south shore of the main river, where it is only some 1,000 yards across, rises Point aux Pères, with Point Lévis nearby.

Although strong in natural situation, Quebec was not invulnerable, particularly from the west: but that was the quarter from which the French considered an attack unlikely. To land an army upstream would face an enemy with two capital difficulties – to get ships past the city, and to do so in the face of artillery fire. Efforts at putting Quebec into a good state of defence had extended over many decades, but few of them had been comprehensive. The most sustained had been made by Governor Beauharnois during the scare which had resulted

from the capture of Louisbourg during the War of the Austrian Succession, at a time when Wolfe was campaigning in Scotland. Quebec had been enclosed on the west by a system of masonry, though it was not very satisfactory.

The most obvious place for an invader to land was where Phips had tried and failed, between the rivers St Charles and Montmorency, in the area which came to be known as Beauport Camp or Lines, named after a village where roads converged. So thought Montcalm, and when he knew that the British were approaching, he acted accordingly. Every available man was brought in, sailors included, to work on a line of defences stretching from Quebec harbour to the Montmorency Falls.

When Bougainville had first returned from France he

A. The Fort.
B. The Recollets.
C. The Platform.
D. The Jesuits.
E. The Cathedral.
F. The Seminary.
G. The Hôtel Dieu.
H. The Bishop's House.
I. The Redoubt.
K. The Hospital.

Eighteenth century Quebec

discovered that Vaudreuil and Montcalm were at Montreal, deciding measures to be taken against an advance of Amherst. After the information brought by the colonel, it was plain that the right place for the grandees was Quebec. Montcalm reached the city on 22 May and Vaudreuil followed two days later. On 12 June Vaudreuil paid his first visit of inspection to the new defences, which gave Montcalm the opportunity to note in his Journal:

M. le Marquis de Vaudreuil, Governor General and in this capacity general of the army, made his first tour; after all, youth must be instructed. As he had never seen either a camp or a work of defence, everything seemed to him as new as it was amusing. He asked singular questions. It was like a man born blind who has been given sight.

Vaudreuil was impressed by the work done, and so, when he found out more about it, was Wolfe. Moreover, an extraordinary mobilisation had been achieved, for which Vaudreuil must be given credit. The figures are uncertain, but a fair estimate is that Vaudreuil and Montcalm had resources in manpower for the defence of Quebec of something over 15,000 men. Their quality, like their ages, varied. There were men of eighty in the ranks, and boys of twelve and thirteen: but from a total available population of about 60,000, it was amazing

Twentieth century Quebec

even when it is considered that a great many Indians had been absorbed.

Two operations were ordered on the river. On 1 June the provision ships were sent over 50 miles upstream to Batiscan where a safe depot of food and munitions was to be established. The effectiveness of this measure depended on control of the river line beyond Quebec, and this was soon in dispute. The alternative of sending material back to Quebec overland in carts was difficult to organise, and was not often attempted. The other measure was the preparation of fireships to send down on the British at night when they were at anchor.

There were fireships in Saunders's fleet, but these were not used at Quebec in the rôle their name suggests. They were, as a class, small, old and expendable, often given to newly promoted officers: for instance, James Chads, once of Howe's *Magnanime*, had charge of the *Vesuvius* in the rank of Master and Commander. The French case was different, and they went to great expense – a million *livres*, some said – to prepare a fireship flotilla which, they hoped, would be as effective as that which had attacked Philip II's Armada off Calais in 1588. The idea was that, shotted and burning, the vessels should drift down with the tide and cause panic and destruction.

It was, however, the sort of attack more likely to be spectacular than effective, especially when used against seasoned people such as were manning Saunders's fleet. There had been no secret about the measures being taken in Quebec, and there was no apprehension on the part of Saunders. Rather, it was perhaps the other way about, for a few weeks earlier, when making ready, one of the eight ships had burned prematurely, nearly causing disaster in the harbour.

On the night of 28 June seven ships ran silently down the river on the tide towards the British, who were anchored in the channel south of the Isle of Orleans. The French officers in charge, no doubt, and justifiably, nervous, fired their ships too soon. The most westerly vessel in Saunders's fleet hastily weighed anchor – the *Centurion* had to cut her cable – and ran for it, firing guns to warn shipping below. Then boats rowed out, grappled the vessels, and coolly towed them clear. Some of the soldiers in the outposts were alarmed, but no harm was done, at a great deal of expense.

They were certainly the grandest fireworks that can possibly be conceived, [wrote Captain Knox] 'every circumstance having contributed to their awful, yet beautiful appearance; the night was serene and calm, there was no light but what the stars produced, and this was eclipsed by the blaze of the floating fires rising from all parts and running about as quick as thought up the masts and rigging.

Quebec and the St Charles River

Soon all seven ships drifted ashore, where each in turn burnt out. Grappling irons had succeeded in turning the one and only French naval attack on any scale into a fiasco. Vaudreuil, looking down at dawn from the city ramparts, found the British ships much as they had been the night before. There had been no casualties on either side, for the French crews had abandoned their vessels in good time – too good, said some of their companions-in-arms.

II

Co-operation between army and navy had so far been exemplary, but relationships did not always continue smooth. There are entries in Wolfe's Journal which show that soon after the arrival of the force at the Isle of Orleans he began to be dissatisfied with the help he was getting: the feeling did not last, and never extended to Saunders, for whom he retained great respect, but there was a time when he even recorded his opinion that certain officers were not as adventurous afloat as he would have wished.

The fact was that, in spite of the failure of the fireships, French gunboats and light craft were bold and well handled. They knew these waters, to which the British came as strangers, and they were actively led. The baneful effects of divided military command did not affect them: all they lacked was numbers. 'The Enemy permitted to insult us with their paltry boats carrying Cannon in their prows,' Wolfe noted indignantly early in July, and he also complained of British frigates and bomb-ketches employed in bombardment duties being 'a prodigious distance from the Enemy.' One of Saunders's problems was Beauport Bank, an expanse of shallows in front of the French position which made it impossible for the fleet to close to effective range. This was an added reason for the soundness of Montcalm's dispositions.

Another naval difficulty (which Wolfe could not appreciate and in any case it was not his business) was that the Quebec Basin, being unknown to Saunders and his captains, was not the easiest place in which to choose the best anchorages for a collection of ships of motley variety. Saunders very soon found this out, for he had no sooner landed the troops than, as he put it in his despatch:

...a very hard Gale of Wind came on, by which many Anchors and small Boats were lost and much damage received among the Transports by their driving on board each other. The Ships that lost most anchors I supplied from the Men of War, as far as I was able, and in all other Respects, gave them the best Assistance in my Power.

Wolfe saw the confusion, and was shocked by it. He did not, perhaps, allow for the fact that the transports, not being naval vessels and sometimes under-manned, were not subject to Saunders's discipline except in general terms, and that many captains were American. The Admiral reported that no less than 27 transports had to be sent to Boston for repair after the storm.

Once Wolfe's army was safely ashore, there developed the inevitable duel of wits and nerves between the opposing commanders. Montcalm knew he had only to delay Wolfe long enough, and Quebec would be reprieved for at least another year, since operations were not possible with ice forming in the river. Wolfe for his part was beginning, even at this early stage,

Brigadier Monckton

to feel the march of time, and it was not in his favour. He was tense and irritable. On his own evidence, only Colonel Carleton's 'great good sense and management' prevented an explosion one day with Captain Mantell of the *Centurion*. And if his task seemed stiff with problems, his health was deteriorating. On 2 July he noted: 'Bladder painful. A good deal racked – studied plans'. There are few ailments more distressing than a disordered bladder, and it was only two days later that Wolfe recorded a 'sad attack of dysentery.'

The French possessed an able naval officer in Jean Vauquelin, a frigate captain who had been appointed 'Commandant of the Road'. Vauquelin's activities caused the cancellation of more than one early plan, including the possibility of a landing

upstream. It was on Saunders's suggestion, made as early as
29 June, that Wolfe decided on two immediate moves from the
Isle of Orleans. One was to make a camp below the Falls of
Montmorency, and the other to occupy Point Lévis. The latter
vantage point had not been fortified, in spite of recommendation by Montcalm, and the area was held by Canadien militia
and Indians. Vaudreuil hesitated to send reinforcements and
guns over from Quebec because a prisoner had stated that any
movements against Point Lévis would be feints, and that the
real pressure would be against the Beauport position. This
tallied with French ideas, and was accepted.

Monckton landed near Point Lévis on 30 June in strength,
mastered the defence, and pushed on towards the heights opposite the city. With ordnance once established there, Quebec
would come under fire in exactly the way that Wolfe forecast
in his letter from sea. So quickly did Monckton operate, in spite
of criticism from Wolfe of some of his arrangements, that by
5 July the city was beginning to suffer, and the process continued.
Later in the month the Cathedral was set on fire and then entirely
gutted as the wind fanned the flames. The garrison's message to
the British after this incident was a brave one: 'We do not
doubt that you will demolish the town, but we are determined
that your army shall never get a footing within its walls.'
Wolfe replied: 'I will be master of Quebec if I stay here until the
end of November.'

Vaudreuil indeed made one desperate effort to dislodge the
British, but it ended farcically and showed how much would
depend on Montcalm's regulars if it came to a set piece battle.
On 11 July a number of citizens drawn from all classes offered
their services to the Governor General for an expedition to seize
the batteries and destroy the British lodgement. After some
hesitation this was agreed to, and command was given to Jean-
Daniel Dumas. He was adjutant-general of the Canadien
regulars, a renowned forest fighter, and, in this instance, a keen
volunteer. The force left Quebec the same night with enthusiastic good wishes, and on the night following crossed the river in
canoes some way above the city, the British being unaware of
what was intended.

The party itself was mixed. It suggested zeal and patriotism

rather than good staff work. Even some schoolboys from the
Jesuit College, often known colloquially as the Royal Syntax,
were included. There was a handful of French regulars and an
Indian advance guard. The idea had been to take up a wooded
position commanding the site of the battery, and to make it
untenable by musketry fire. As the scheme involved a night
march across broken country towards what could have been an
alert and strong opposition, planning and organisation would
need to be meticulous to offer much chance of success.

As the expedition moved towards its objective it fell into
disorder, and it was not long before members were mistaking
their own people for the British. Shots were exchanged,
casualties suffered. Dumas tried to rally his men three times, but
on each occasion there was undisciplined firing against an enemy
who was not there. In the end most of the party rushed downhill
to the river, eager to get back to the canoes. Only the Indians

The Montmorency Falls

performed with any skill, but when they returned to report that the British were quiet and unsuspecting, they found that the situation among the pale-faces was beyond recovery. By dawn on 14 July the whole force was back on the north shore, leaving a few corpses killed by French bullets in the woods. It was five days before Wolfe heard the story from a deserter.

Wolfe himself was by this time established on the north shore of the St Lawrence, east of Montmorency Falls, with Townshend's and Murray's brigades encamped nearby. The crossings from the Isle of Orleans had been made without opposition, and the main forces of each side now faced each other across the Montmorency River. French pilots had asserted that it would be impossible for ships of any size to use what was known as the Montmorency or North Channel, but this was shown to be nonsense.

The Channel itself was surveyed by Cook, after which the frigate *Halifax* and the *Porcupine* sloop-of-war managed to work their way into it, to safeguard the crossing. Two ships were stationed off the beach, their boats being the only means of communication with the camp on the Island. John Jervis, Master and Commander, was in charge of the *Porcupine*, for Saunders had taken the opportunity to promote the zealous officer – he was then twenty-four – who had been first lieutenant of the *Neptune*. Jervis and Wolfe had sat under the same schoolmaster at Greenwich, though not at the same time, and a friendship between them had been established during the Atlantic crossing.

Wolfe made his headquarters in a house in the area of the Falls, where he lived in such state as his position required. He was attended by his servant, François, who had been with him some years, and three footmen. He dined off plate, which he was to bequeath to Saunders 'in remembrance of his guest' – an indication of their friendliness. His forces were now divided – very much like his own ideas. Monckton was opposite the city. The bulk of the army was under the eye of the general, and there was a stores depot and a hospital, with light forces guarding them, near West Point on the Isle of Orleans.

Wolfe would perhaps have felt the need of advice from someone at least as experienced in war as himself, but older.

At Louisbourg there had been Amherst to take the burden of responsibility. At Quebec Wolfe seems to have considered, as Nelson did later, that Councils of War did little but decide to do nothing. He consulted rarely, and then mainly with Saunders, who though unfamiliar with purely military problems was a man of sense, not in the least laggardly, even if some of his subordinates appeared to be, and of a riper age than Wolfe. The general had, perhaps, been righter than he realised when he made a show of reluctance to assume chief command in such a complex undertaking. Even Saunders had to make allowances more than once for petulance and complaints. He did so consistently, refusing to be huffed, though never allowing criticism of the Navy, merited or not, to go on official record. He was at all times willing to go more than half way to help the Army. No man could have done more, and few admirals of that era would have done as much.

III

Ever since the first landings there had been skirmishings in the woods, in which the Canadiens usually had the advantage. They were expert at outpost work, and so were their Indian allies, who were out for scalps. A scalped head on a murdered man is not a pretty sight, and sentries in lonely posts grew nervous.

Foraging parties had already encountered ambushes, in which the Indians specialised. A platoon of Rangers had been early sufferers when they established a post on the south bank upstream, near the confluence of the river Etchemin with the St Lawrence. They had nine men scalped, but the Rangers themselves could be savage. Colonel Fraser of the Highland regiment reported in shocked words how they killed the children of some peasants they were bringing in prisoners, for fear that their cries should give away their own position. 'The wretches boasted of it on their return,' wrote Fraser, 'though they now pretend to vindicate themselves by the necessity they were under; but I believe this barbarous action proceeded from the cowardice and barbarity which seems so natural to a native of America, whether of Indian or European extraction.'

There were various ways in which Wolfe's own men could be braced against panic, not by flogging, which was practised as mercilessly in the army of the 18th century as the navy, but, sometimes at least, by ridicule. Two private soldiers found this out when they were punished for showing alarm about nothing. As they had –

... behaved in a scandalous and unsoldierlike manner upon their post, the first screaming out and firing his piece and both by giving the most evident tokens of fear, it is the Colonel's orders that they shall stand an hour at the necessary house [latrine] each with a woman's cap upon his head as a small punishment for the dishonour they have brought upon the Corps and their brother soldiers. They are in future to march in the front of all parties without a grain of powder in their pieces, where they may have the opportunity to wipe off the infamy they now lie under.

One of the problems, before the nature and direction of a full scale attack on the French had been decided, was to keep the men occupied profitably. It was soon realised that if, as seemed likely, an assault on the Beauport Lines was to be mounted, rafts would be necessary to negotiate the shelving flats in front of the French position. Some were made as a matter of urgency, and a massive artillery park was also assembled at the Montmorency Camp, since Wolfe knew that in this particular arm his preponderance was considerable, and he hoped to exploit it. It was noticeable that in the exchanges between the batteries near Point Lévis and those in Quebec, French gunners replied sparingly. They were conserving ammunition, of which they had a limited supply. There was plenty in the British ships.

The shape of the rafts differed entirely from that of the flat-bottomed boats with which the fleet was equipped. They were designed to carry 300 men. Their decks were supported by casks lashed together. Hand rails ran round three sides, the fourth having a bullet-proof shield. This formed a ramp which could be lowered when the raft was beached. The difficulty was propulsion: oars could move the rafts only slowly and clumsily, and there is no evidence that the new constructions were ever used.

In this particular line, it was the French who acted. They were

The Church of Notre Dame

determined to make one more effort to burn the British fleet. On the night of 27/28 July a great mass of rafts and small craft chained together was sent down the river. This time there was no premature combustion, and the officer in charge, M. de Courval, did his work well. He waited until the mass was close to a concentration of shipping before setting fire to it, but the operation was not supported by French gun-boats, as had been planned – the keen edge of earlier zest was wearing thin in the face of numerical superiority – and the boats were once again able to tow the flaming menace out of harm's way, without difficulty and without loss. The log of the *Stirling Castle*, at that time Saunders's flagship, recorded briefly: 'Serv'd the boatmen for the above service $\frac{1}{2}$ a pint of brandy each.' Surely the men deserved it.

By this time the city of Quebec had begun to suffer badly and was partly evacuated. Vaudreuil suspected that an attempt might be made to assault the Lower Town, though Mackellar had reported this to be impracticable. Personal casualties from 'carcasses' or incendiary projectiles were light, but structures suffered badly. One of those hit most repeatedly was the

Ah, Monsieur le Generale si Quebec tombe — Votre Altesse épargnerez
les femmes?
Celà depend, mes bonnes — plus des Petitions écrites. Dépêchez
50 belles vierges toute de suite à Moi — et nous verrons!

Townshend's caricature of Wolfe and two Frenchwomen

Ursuline Convent, a conspicuous building in the centre of the
Upper Town. On one occasion the nuns passed most of a night
'before the Blessed Sacrament, in such terrors as may be
imagined.' Next morning their Superior led them to the safety
of the General Hospital on the river St Charles, north west of
the city. In one bombardment during August, 152 houses were

reduced to ashes and the Church of Notre Dame des Victoires was burnt out.

Some weeks earlier the invaluable Carleton had gone upstream to Pointe aux Trembles, twenty miles from Quebec, skirmished with a party of Indians, and returned with civilian prisoners. They included women, who were later sent over to the city under a flag of truce. They were full of praise for the treatment they had received. Some of them had even dined with Wolfe, who had jested a good deal, in his ready French, about Montcalm's circumspection. On 21 July Rear Admiral Holmes went above Quebec by land, with an escort, and hoisted his flag on board the *Sutherland*.

This ship of the line was able to make her way upstream on the night of 18/19 July, in company with *Squirrel* frigate, two sloops of war, and two transports. The little force went up, wind and tide serving, in the face of concentrated fire, without losing a man, though the *Sutherland* had one shot just above the water-line which did no harm. A second frigate, the *Diana*, had bad luck: She was fouled by one of the sloops, and ran aground on the south shore opposite the town. This was a chance for the French gun-boat commanders to show what they were made of. Five of them attacked her, but after jettisoning most of her guns, the *Diana* was got off the next day with the help of the *Pembroke*, *Richmond* and numerous boats.

The advent of a very senior officer upstream, in command of ships of size, which could be reinforced when the wind was right, was a great success for the British, for whether or not a landing beyond Quebec was attempted, Holmes could now intercept supplies trying to reach the city by water, and immobilise the French frigates higher up. Wolfe himself was quick to pursue the advantage, for he made a personal reconnaissance the day the *Diana* got off, and concluded that if he had made an attempt from the west earlier, an idea with which he had toyed, he would have succeeded in establishing a position which he could have entrenched. 'General cheerful' recorded Captain Bell, who was with him. He did not stay long in this condition, for the French reacted quickly.

The *Sutherland* and the other ships had first anchored near the Anse des Mères, scarcely a mile from Cape Diamond. Dumas

French fireships at Quebec

was sent there with 600 men, including some Indians and a cavalry unit which Montcalm had formed earlier in the year. Batteries were placed which could shell the anchorage, and the gunners soon made it too hot for the sailors. The *Squirrel* was hit in a mast and in her rigging, and was towed higher up out of range.

IV

Although Wolfe appeared to have the initiative and undoubtedly had the means to move where and when he wished about the perimeter of the French position, he seemed everywhere frustrated. He made one plan after another, and time after time they were cancelled – often on the same day. He could now even land on the north shore above Quebec, though not in force until more shipping had run the gauntlet of the city batteries, and certainly not without opposition.

He tried a reconnaissance in strength up the river Montmorency, to a ford three miles from his camp. His idea was that if he could cross there, he might be able to advance west to the line of the St Charles and perhaps threaten Quebec from the rear.

The French had anticipated such a move. Montcalm and de Lévis had watched from a distance the landing of Townshend's

18th c tomahawk sold by the British to the Indians

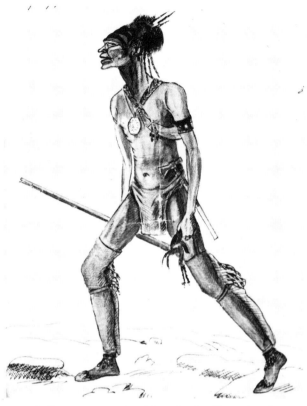

Indian on warpath with scalp, by Townshend

situation did not alarm him, for a believed there was no ford higher up the river, while a crossing below the Falls, which was negotiable only at low tide, could be commanded from the Beauport positions. A local militiaman, overhearing this, whispered to Chevalier Johnstone, the Jacobite ADC, that the general was wrong: there *was* a practical ford, and he produced a man who had used it the previous night.

A party of Indians was thereupon organised to cross it, and to harass the vanguard of the sortie. They attacked some Rangers they encountered in the woods and were bloodily repulsed – for the Rangers were expert in their own sort of fighting, and not above scalping. When they had news of this, Montcalm and de Lévis decided against taking any further action except to defend their own side of the river in the neighbourhood of the crossing. Montcalm also vetoed a direct attack on Wolfe's camp. 'Drive them from thence,' he remarked, 'and they will give us more trouble. While they are there they cannot hurt us: let them amuse themselves.'

Wolfe's move brought about one other fierce skirmish, after which Captain Bell reported that he 'got his arm broke by the Rascals. We had about 45 men killed and wounded.' Wolfe had two battalions with him. One of them was Howe's Light Infantry, recently brought over from the Isle of Orleans. They found the French firmly entrenched on the other side of the ford, where the river bank was steep and woody. Wolfe withdrew.

As the Montmorency idea seemed doomed, there seemed nothing for it but an assault on the Beauport Lines. Wolfe had his eye on a redoubt near the shore which he hoped would, if captured, give him a point of vantage from which to see what the French were doing. Far more important, such an exploit, if successful, might tempt Montcalm to try to dislodge him. That was what Wolfe most wanted, for he reckoned that he would be able to reinforce the defenders at any time the redoubt was in serious danger. When brought to battle he had no doubt of the superior quality of his own troops, and they were eager to justify themselves.

Certainly the army expected something. The expedition had already been a month in front of Quebec, and Wolfe had found fault with almost everyone, Townshend particularly. Townshend was offended to such a degree by Wolfe's attitude towards him that on 13 July he noted indignantly that the general set off for Point Lévis without giving him any direction or indication of his probable movements. Adept with his brush and pencil, the brigadier was less polished with his pen, but the account he set down of what happened when he hurried after Wolfe to the beach to request information is charged with feeling, and shows all too well the state of their relationship.

He received me in a very stately manner, not advancing five steps; I told him if I had suspected his intention of going over I had waited on him for his Commands which I should be glad to receive and execute to his satisfaction. Sir says he very drily the Adjutant General has my orders, permit me Sir to ask are ye Troops to encamp now on their new ground or not to do it until ye Enemies Battery begins to play?

Matters did not mend after Wolfe announced his intention to make an attempt to take the redoubt, for none of the brigadiers liked the idea, and they said so. However, as they themselves could suggest nothing better, it went ahead.

The first attack would be by grenadiers, picked men, who would be reinforced from Monckton's camp across the St. Lawrence. They would be helped by gunfire from ships brought as close inshore as possible. When the state of the tide enabled them to ford the Montmorency below the Falls, Townshend's and Murray's brigades would advance to the French side, covered by the artillery which Wolfe had massed near his camp, and by guns from seaward. Wolfe noted in his Journal: 'Possibility of a general engagement on attack from us – preparations for it.' This was to prove altogether too sanguine, but it had been the hope behind the plan from the start.

The original date settled on was 30 July, and everyone was alerted, but a flat calm made naval movements impossible. The next day was clear and very hot, but with enough breeze for the ships, so the operation was put in motion. The *Centurion*, with Saunders once more on board ship he knew so well when younger, moved into the Montmorency Channel, ready to bombard the batteries on Montcalm's extreme left, one of which formed part of the redoubt.

Cook had made a report on the area of fore-shore to be used, but this had necessarily to be little more than guesswork, since, being subject to direct fire, boats could not go in to take accurate soundings. For once, his calculation proved more cheerful than exact, for the bombardment vessels ('catts' was the term used, and it indicated a bluff wide bow and shallow draft), which were to give covering fire to the landing, could not get in as close as Wolfe had hoped, and their shooting was not very effective. Distance was against them, and the gunners could not elevate their pieces sufficiently to threaten the higher positions held by the enemy.

The ships, the *Russell* and *Three Sisters*, duly ran in, Wolfe being on board the *Russell*, to get a close look at the French. The enemy was thoroughly prepared, and opened a heavy fire.

Contemporary models of H.M.S. Centurion . . .

'I was no less than three times struck with splinters,' Wolfe later wrote to Saunders, 'and had my stick knocked out of my hand with a cannonball.' As usual, he was at his best in danger, which acted on him like a tonic.

From his view-point on board, Wolfe saw at once what no inspection more distant could have told him – that the redoubt was much nearer to the French entrenchments along the heights than it had appeared to be. Further, it was clear that, even if captured, it would not be tenable. Yet to countermand the whole operation when the Navy was already in action, and troops ready to embark, would have appeared so faint-hearted as to have had a shattering effect on morale.

After some time, Wolfe noticed that the defenders of the redoubt appeared to be becoming disorganised. The fact, if it was a fact, decided him. The *Russell* and *Three Sisters* had gone in about 11 o'clock. An hour and a half later, the boats with the landing parties put off from the Isle of Orleans, and lay in the Montmorency Channel near the *Centurion* under spasmodic artillery fire, awaiting further orders. When at last they were sent in they met with trouble from obstacles under water such as ledges of rock on which some of them grounded.

The attack was temporarily halted. Then an officer was ordered to warn Townshend, and Wolfe himself, at Saunders's suggestion, went with a naval officer in a flat-bottomed boat to find a suitable spot for the men to land. Much time had been lost, so that it was not until half past five, with the sky full of thunder clouds, that grenadiers made for the place Wolfe had chosen.

Thirteen companies of grenadiers and 200 men of the Royal Americans led the assault. They went in waist deep, and so recklessly as to invite trouble. Wolfe ordered the Grenadiers March to beat, and this, as one of the few surviving officers reported, 'animated our Men so much that we could scarce restrain them.' The companies, instead of forming up in an orderly way on the beach and waiting for Monckton's battalions to strengthen them, made a wild dash for the enemy. The eyes

. . . and a flat bottomed landing craft

of their comrades-in-arms were on them and they were determined, after their nerve-wracking wait, to show what they
could do.

This was fatal, for although the French left the redoubt, a
shattering fire came from the entrenchments above. The
British were sitting targets. The men made an attempt to rush
the slopes, but they were too steep and they were slaughtered.

At this critical moment, Nature took a hand. One of the
violent summer storms, characteristic of this part of Canada,
suddenly burst, and the rain quickly soaked all the gunpowder,
of which, incidentally, the French had little left. The tide was
now at a stage when it would be difficult for the troops from
Montmorency to re-cross the ford unless they were ordered to
do so at once, and this was done. Some companies of Fraser's
Highlanders formed the rearguard, and Wolfe marched with
them. Other Highlanders were with Monckton.

Those of Monckton's force who had landed were taken off,
together with the survivors of the grenadiers and Royal
Americans, but not until they knew that all their clansmen were
safe would the Highlanders cross the ford. By that time, noted
Townshend, 'ye tide of flood was so high that the Regiments
could scarcely wade over.'

The *Russell* and *Three Sisters* had been damaged past repair.
The crews were taken off and the vessels burnt. Wolfe returned
a loss of 210 killed and 230 wounded as the bill for a sorry day's
work. Among the killed was Sergeant Ned Botwood of the
47th Regiment, a spirited and popular bard who had promised
'Hot Stuff' to the enemy. Alas, it was he himself who received it.

How right the Highlanders had been to be sure that all their
own men were taken off is illustrated by what happened to two
officers of the Royal Americans. Some wounded were left on
the beach, and as soon as the boats got away, Indians descended
with war whoops, tomahawks and scalping knives. Captain
Ochterlony and Lieutenant Peyton were such devoted friends
that when a Highlander had offered to carry one of the two off
on his shoulders they refused to be parted. Peyton, with
enormous skill and courage, held off the redskin who attacked
him, but Ochterlony was only saved from another by the
intervention of a French officer who seized the Indian's arm

just as he was about to strike. Ochterlony was taken to a hospital in Quebec, where he died a few days later. Wolfe sent the French officer a reward of £20, but Montcalm returned the money, saying that the act had only been in the way of duty. It would be good to think that such chivalry could have extended to other ranks, but if it did, there is no record of it.

V

Montcalm had been left in no doubt of the serious nature of the Montmorency attack. The dreadful relics lay strewn on the fore-shore, and he had seen with his own eyes that all the main British forces had been involved. Although not complacent, he had remained serene, and justifiably so. He had not even taken personal charge of the defence.

Vaudreuil had been at his headquarters near the St. Charles throughout, complaining later that he heard simultaneously of the British attack and re-embarkation, though it is hard to believe that with firing so continuous and concentrated he did not know that something unusual was taking place. de Lévis, so the Governor General was told, had taken immediate charge and done well. Montcalm had only visited his subordinate once, and then moved westwards to make sure that other positions could not be taken by surprise. This merely showed that the general was not unduly worried, and that he trusted de Lévis.

Vaudreuil afterwards wrote to Brigadier Bourlamaque, who was facing Amherst, saying that he had no anxiety now for any front except that of the St. Lawrence rapids, facing Lake Ontario. Montcalm, more cautious and experienced, also wrote, but in different terms. He suggested that the 'affair' was 'a small prelude to something more important, which we are now waiting for.' As so often, he was right, but there would be a long wait, for Wolfe was thwarted, and very angry. In his more searching moments he did not blame anyone more than himself. He faced criticism, some of it open and unexpected, as in the case of Carleton, some sly. In an age when elaborate investigations following miscarriages were the rule, there was talk of a Parliamentary enquiry being likely. This was designed to make the general still more edgy, though in fact that was scarcely possible. What was absent was an atmosphere in the camps that, if the attack had been a failure, all the more reason for encouraging Wolfe to try something better. His losses, though sad, were not crippling, and the Navy retained and was increasing its ascendancy.

Wolfe's reproof to the troops was in sharp terms, and caused some grumbling among the rank and file, on whose loyalty Wolfe depended now more than ever.

The check which the grenadiers met with yesterday, [he wrote] will, it is hoped, be a lesson to them for the time to come: such impetuous, irregular and unsoldierlike proceedings destroy all order, make it impossible for their Commanders to form any disposition for an attack, and put it out of the General's power to execute his plan.

One of the sailors, Pat Gibson, went on record as saying that 'this cruel aspersion has disgusted every man who was an eye-witness of such gallantry': nevertheless, Wolfe's reputation had been founded on firm control of troops in battle and it was essential to emphasise the importance of discipline. The lesson was salutary, and it was digested. The one compensation in the attack was not, and could not, have been perceived by the British. It convinced Montcalm more firmly than ever that Wolfe's eye was on Beauport, whatever moves he might make elsewhere. This had a great effect during the final stages of the campaign, so much so that the grenadiers and Royal Americans did not die in vain.

In a draft despatch about the engagement, Wolfe reflected on the ineffectiveness of the naval bombardment, due to the fact that the ships were too far away. Naturally enough, Saunders objected to any strictures on his Service, and Wolfe agreed to remove the offending sentence, although he insisted privately that the facts were as he had stated them. The letter in which he promised an amendment was in a tone of humility which must have touched Saunders. 'I am sensible,' said the general 'of my own errors in the course of the campaign, see clearly wherein I have been deficient; and think a little more or less blame to a man that must necessarily be ruined of little consequence.' He summed up: 'The blame I take entirely upon my own shoulders,

Cartoon by Townshend

and I expect to suffer for it. Accidents cannot be helped . . . A man sees his errors often too late to remedy.'

One character who saw these errors plainly, and rubbed them in, was Townshend. This is not speculation, for the brigadier left evidence on the subject, both written and drawn. Wolfe had begun a policy of devastation of the countryside in the belief that it would cause Canadian militiamen to desert, when, as they so often were to do, they saw smoke from burning farms making dark clouds in the distant sky. This form of warfare was detestable, and Townshend, for one, loathed it. Moreover, he had had a loss which brought the matter home to him sharply. His brother had died in Canada while with Amherst's army.

'I never serv'd so disagreeable a Campaign,' he told his wife. 'Our unequal Force has reduced our Operations to a scene of Skirmishing, Cruelty and Devastation. It is War of the worst shape. A Scene I ought not to be in, for the future believe me my dear Charlotte I will seek the reverse of it . . . Genl. Wolf's Health is but very bad. His Generalship in my poor opinion is not a bit better, this only between *us*.' But that is just what Townshend's criticism of Wolfe was not – a private matter.

The officer's messes in the Montmorency Camp were soon amusedly aware of Townshend's versatility as an artist. He had already shown how well he could catch a straight likeness. Now he turned satirist, and the results were at once gross, insubordinate and funny. There were two types of drawing, a finished and elegant sort, such as Max Beerbohm could have produced, but with indecent subject, and rough pen and ink sketches, with no holds barred. One of these showed Isaac Barré, the Adjutant General, measuring Wolfe. It was captioned: '*Higher than before! Our Generall begins his day.*'

Wolfe's note-taking staff-officer wrote about Townshend that he was of:

. . . an inconstant mind, his line of life not directed by any first principles, and as he is exceedingly subject to very high and low spirits, his actions have a variegated colour, one while the appearance of excess of good nature, at other times of Bitterness, and as his favours are not directed by merit, he is always surrounded by the most indifferent subjects in the Army. He has a great deal of humour, well stained with bawdy, and may be esteemed an excellent Tavern acquaintance.

This entirely disregards Townshend's more respectable gifts and qualities, which were considerable, but of the effect of his cartoons there can be no doubt. They tended to undermine confidence at the very time when it most needed building up, and they were criminally irresponsible as coming from the third

Townshend in later life

in military command. But the man who presumed to satirise Wolfe was the same person who, as a stripling, had dared to criticise His Majesty King George II when he felt the sovereign was making nonsense of his soldiers' success at Dettingen.

Some of the cartoons have been preserved, and one at least found its way to Amherst. Doubtless there were others. Wolfe himself is said to have encountered a specimen, which he angrily crumpled, remarking that more would be heard of the matter. It could have led to a duel, but meanwhile there were other things to consider than the results of the malice of an officer who, to be fair, had had no opportunity so far during the campaign to prove his own qualities of leadership. Monckton from the first had had what was almost an independent command opposite Quebec. The sharp-featured Murray was soon to be sent upstream on a foray which might be of great consequence. Townshend was left at what he wrote of as the 'cursed Camp of Montmorencie' to stew in his own gravy. That in itself was something of a penance.

Murray's mission had various objects, all of them sensible and important, and it was planned in close consultation with Saunders, since Rear Admiral Holmes was involved. Wolfe put the matter succinctly in the last despatch he sent home to Pitt. There were French ships higher up the St. Lawrence, including the frigates which had arrived with Bougainville soon after the previous year's ice had broken. Although many of the sailors had been taken off to serve the guns of Quebec, the frigates were between Wolfe and Amherst, and they constituted a threat to any British naval force which might be left in the St. Lawrence after Saunders, with the bigger vessels, had departed for home.

Wolfe told Pitt that Murray had been directed to help Rear Admiral Holmes 'in the Destruction of the French ships (if they could be got at) in order to open a Communication with General Amherst. The Brigadier was to seek every favourable opportunity of fighting some of the Enemy's Detachments, provided he could do it upon tolerable Terms, and to use all the Means in his Power to provoke them to attack him.' This was a proposal to Murray's liking. It gave him the chance to act on his own, and he set about his task with zest. All the signs were that August would be a gloomy month for those in and around the Quebec Basin, and Murray's relief at this chance of escape was scarcely disguised. His officers and men felt much as he did.

Murray went off with about 1,200 men during the first day of the month, and Montcalm took appropriate counter-measures. He reinforced his posts above the city so that the total under arms was about 1,000, including all the mounted infantry. He put Bougainville in command, and there the colonel was to stay until the campaign was over.

There were marines and sailors involved under Murray, and one of the first operations was an attempt to land at Pointe Aux Trembles, about 200 miles above Quebec, 'to favour the Seamen in cutting off three floating Batteries which lay on the north shore.' The first effort was frustrated by rocks. The second, made at high water, was beaten off by Bougainville's fire. Murray and Holmes suffered a good many casualties, including thirty sailors. The Brigadier then sent word back to Wolfe on the 9th that 'the Ship Scheme won't do,' after which he landed his force at St. Antoine, opposite Pointe aux Trembles, in the face of some opposition from Canadians and Indians.

On 18 August Holmes and Murray went higher, using the boats by night, and attacked Deschambault, on the north shore, where spare equipment and baggage for the French regular battalions was stored. The depot and its contents were burned. The rest of a lively and successful day was 'employ'd', so Murray reported, 'in destroying all that could be of service to the Enemy, and in skirmishing with the French force, Dragoons and Indians.' They kept their distance, Murray added, through 'the dread they had of the English Musket.' Bougainville himself only arrived, with his main body, as the raiders were re-embarking.

This event so alarmed Montcalm, as a threat to his communications, that he left Quebec in person with his grenadiers to join Bougainville. On his way he heard that Murray had withdrawn, so he returned to Beauport.

Wolfe thought that Murray had been away long enough, and sent urgent messages for his recall, though the Brigadier did not reach Point Lévis until 25 August. But he brought good news, first of his own modest success, and then, through prisoners, of Amherst. Far away to the west, Fort Niagara had fallen, after a French relieving force had been defeated. Brigadier Prideaux, who had conducted the siege, had been killed in action, but his work had been taken over by Sir William Johnson, who had carried it through.

Montcalm had known this news much earlier, on 9 August, and had taken what steps he could to meet the crisis. He had sent de Lévis off to take command of the sector concerned. With him went 800 men from the Quebec army. Such a detachment,

Brigadier Murray

the general wrote grimly to Bourlamaque, was a great sub-
traction 'from a little force obliged to keep watch from Jacques
Cartier to Montmorency Falls.' Montcalm himself took over at
de Lévis's old post, opposite Wolfe's camp, where he believed
the main threat still to lie.

Wolfe was to have no direct news from Amherst for some
time yet. Bourlamaque had abandoned Ticonderoga to him,
but Amherst did not exploit the situation, contenting himself
by building a flotilla for use on Lake Champlain, and not
attempting to push on towards Wolfe. He was no quicker over
his movements than he had been at Louisbourg.

VI

For a full week, between 19 August and the day of Murray's return, Wolfe was laid up with fever. Judging by his recorded appearance, he may well have been consumptive: he had already referred to bladder and rheumatic troubles, and he was now justifiably depressed. Murray, for all he knew, might have been defeated; Townshend was no friend, and Wolfe seems to have disturbed even the equable Monckton, though the cloud does not seem to have lasted long, and only casual references to the matter recur in the general's Journal. But there was always Saunders, staunch, reserved, but understanding, and the admiral was now busy sending ships up the river by night, or, if the wind did not serve, and it was westerly for most of the month, flat-bottomed boats. The admiral's despatches record that on 5 August he sent up twenty for Murray's use with his expedition. On 27 August the frigate *Lowestoft*, three sloops, including the *Hunter*, and two transport and provision ships, got up on a fourth attempt. Two days later they were joined by the *Seahorse* frigate, by two further sloops and two more transports.

On 4 September all the rest of the flat-bottomed boats were sent, and as they were to play a great part in the final moves, it is fortunate that a description of how they were manned is extant, deriving from less than three years later, when a similar expedition against Havana was preparing. It was then that Anson made one of his last excursions from London. This was to Portsmouth, to see the regiments embark. The party included Prince Charles of Mecklenberg, Lord Albemarle and Admiral Pocock, who were the military and naval commanders-in-chief, and two veterans of Quebec, Colonels Carleton and Howe. A gentleman in the Prince's entourage, Frederick Kielmansegge, later published a diary of his visit to England, and he offered the following account:

Since the beginning of this war the English have very much accelerated the embarkation and disembarkation of troops by inventing for the purpose a kind of flat boat; in which my Lord Howe has taken a considerable part. These boats are arranged for fifty or sixty men; their shape is somewhat similar to that of the long boats which men-of-war generally carry, but they are much larger and have flat bottoms for the purpose of getting closer into shore.

All of these flat boats, each of which has twenty to twenty-one oars, were lying in one row along the shore, and as soon as the regiment had marched past it formed up again close to the shore, and awaited the signal for entering the boats. Immediately on this being given, each officer marched with his men to the boat, of which he had previously received the number; then he and his drummer entered first and passed right through from the bows onshore to the stern, the whole division following him without breaking their ranks; so that in two minutes everybody was in the boats.

The officers and drummers, with their corporals sit aft near the rudder, the privates in two or three rows behind one another on the thwarts, holding their muskets before them, and two petty officers sit in the bows, so as not to be hampered in the use of their oars. As soon as everything has been arranged in this way, the naval officer commanding the embarkation gives a signal, when all the boats start off at the same time and row to their respective vessels.

If Saunders was employed, during the time of Wolfe's indisposition, in getting a greater concentration of shipping and boats upstream, it is unlikely that the general, even when entirely confined to his room at Montmorency, was idle. An incessant reader, who put his assiduity to good use, military history was his speciality, and he extended his detailed knowledge back to classical times. Yet he was anything but narrow in his tastes, and he liked poetry. There is some reason to suppose that he may have been in the toils of literary composition at this very time, and he certainly knew and admired Gray's *Elegy*, for a copy given him by Katherine Lowther, with favourite passages marked, survived.

Perhaps the best known story about Wolfe is that on his way to his last battle he repeated nearly the whole of Gray's stanzas, '. . . adding, as he concluded, that he would prefer being the author of that poem to the glory of beating the French tomorrow.'

There may be some truth behind the tale, which derived from the recollections in old age of John Robison, who had been present as a youth with the expedition. All the same, it does not accord with the certain knowledge that the paramount object of Wolfe's life was victory in battle.

About his thoughts on this subject there is evidence from some lines Wolfe transcribed from Pope's translation of the 12th book of the *Iliad*, with some variations of his own. They read:

> But since, alas! ignoble age must come,
> Disease, and death's inexorable doom,
> The life which others pay, let us bestow,
> And give to Fame, what we to nature owe.
> Brave let us fall, or honoured if we live,
> Or let us glory gain, or glory give.
> Such, men shall own, deserve a sovereign state,
> Envied by those who dare not imitate.

PART FOUR

THE PATH TO GLORY

The new plan · The landing
The battle · Townshend's predicament
Hope for the French · Final victory

THE PATH TO GLORY

I

SEPTEMBER brought a change in affairs which was most significant. Wolfe began to recover, by no means completely, for his health was beyond that, 'ruined,' was his own word, but enough to compose a despatch to Pitt, which he superscribed the 2nd of the month. This gave the Minister a summary, gloomy in tone, of what had gone before. The missive, and a despatch from Saunders, went off by the *Rodney* cutter. The admiral was more cheerful: he told Pitt:

. . . the Enemy appear numerous, and seem to be strongly posted; but let the Event be what it will, we shall remain here as long as the Season of the Year will permit, in order to prevent their detaching Troops from hence against General Amherst; and I shall leave Cruisers at the Mouth of the River to cut off any Supplies that may be sent them, with strict Orders to keep that station as long as possible.

Saunders intended no repetition of Durell's miscarriage, and he added: 'the Town of Quebec is not habitable, being almost entirely burnt and destroyed.' Montcalm used almost the same words a few days later.

The essential change which had come over the high command was that, at last, Wolfe was prepared to consult his brigadiers, and to take their advice. There was nothing more to be done, in earnest at any rate, by way of attack on the Beauport Lines – of that, all but Wolfe seem now to have felt sure. But with Monckton's batteries ever more oppressively dominating the city, there was little risk in getting ships upstream, and there are indications that Saunders, in his quiet way, was beginning to anticipate how a climax could be brought about. What was lacking, all too often, was what the French called a 'British wind' – from the easterly direction – but even this came sometimes.

During the last few days of August, with Murray available for consultation, Wolfe had begged 'the Brigadiers will be so good [as] to meet, & consult together for the publick utility & advantage; & to consider of the best method of attacking the Enemy.' He added prophetically: 'if the French army is attacked & defeated, the General concludes the Town wou'd immediately surrender, because he does not find they have any Provisions in the Place.' This information had been obtained from deserters, of whom there was always a flow.

Wolfe suggested for consideration ideas for attacks on the Beauport Lines: they included an encircling march to take Montcalm in the rear, such as had led to the skirmish when he reconnoitred the Montmorency river; or a march across the passage below the Falls to probe the French positions; or a variation of the second plan, with the addition of frontal attacks from the St. Lawrence. None of them were acceptable. The lessons of 31 July were too recent, and the position at Beauport had in no way changed, as to some degree it had elsewhere. The brigadiers suggested instead that the army should be brought to the south shore of the main river, 'and to direct the Operations above the Town.'

If such a course was taken, so ran the argument, Montcalm must fight on British terms, for any engagement would be fought 'betwixt him and his provisions, and betwixt him and their Army opposing General Amherst.' Pressing home the point, they added that if Montcalm gave battle and lost, 'Quebec must be ours, and which is more all Canada must submit to His Majesty's arms, a different Case from any advantage we can hope for at Beauport.' They meant that even if Montcalm was defeated at Beauport, it would not prevent him from withdrawing to the interior of New France and prolonging the struggle. On the other hand, a landing above the city would trap the French and settle the matter there and then.

The brigadiers concluded, with becoming deference, that they could not 'presume to advise' on the timing of the operation, and they ended by assuring Wolfe that 'whatever he determines to do, he will find us most hearty, and Zealous in the execution of his Orders.' Wisely, they had taken Saunders fully into their counsel. They spent nearly two days on board the

Stirling Castle with the admiral. Townshend and Murray were actually his guests overnight. At mid-day on 30 August all three military officers left the flagship for Wolfe's headquarters at Montmorency Camp, where they put their memorandum before him.

Wolfe wasted no time in making sure that Saunders approved. He conferred with his naval colleague ashore on 31 August, and next day orders were given to withdraw from the Montmorency Camp. The main body was to cross to Point Lévis, but establishments on the Isle of Orleans were to be maintained.

Wolfe made one last attempt to induce Montcalm to attack him by laying a trap. After moving away the guns and many troops, he still left five battalions behind. 'Great silence is to be preserved,' he enjoined, 'and not a man to show himself on any account, but to lie conceal'd in their Posts to try once more if the Enemy would attack us.' Montcalm, that 'wary old fox', as Wolfe sometimes described him, was not playing. Townshend thereupon supervised the final withdrawal, with Monckton making a feint from Point Lévis on the right of the French position. The way was now clear for a complete change of direction.

Orders were issued on 4 September for the moves which were planned to take place above Quebec. Murray marched from Point Lévis with four line battalions, the Light Infantry and the Louisbourg Grenadiers, crossed the Etchemin River on the south shore, near posts established by Captain Gorham of the Rangers, and the troops then embarked in the ships above the town. They were joined by others under Monckton and Townshend.

The weather now took a hand, and it poured. This was most uncomfortable for the soldiers packed in the transports. Wolfe and his brigadiers were luckier, for at least they could go up and down the river freely, rain or not, so that Wolfe could decide on a place for the landings. He had written to his mother (addressing her formally as 'Dear Madam') as soon as he had agreed to the new strategy. It was for the last time, and he put his difficulties clearly before her:

The Enemy puts nothing to Risk, & I can't in conscience put the whole Army to Risk. My Antagonist has wisely shut himself up in inacessible Entrenchments, so that I can't get at him without spilling a Torrent of blood, and that perhaps to little Purpose.

The Marquis de Montcalm is at the Head of a great number of bad Soldiers, and I am at the Head of a small number of good ones, that wish for nothing so much as to Fight him – but the wary old fellow avoids an Action, doubtful of the Behaviour of his Army. People must be of the Profession to understand the Disadvantages & Difficulties we labour under, arising from the uncommon Natural Strength of the Country.

He also told her of his intention to quit the service at the first opportunity, partly perhaps to assure her that, after the death of his father, she need not feel herself too much alone. Meanwhile, it fell to him to decide just where the 'uncommon Natural Strength of the Country' offered the best opening, and by 9 or 10 September he seems to have made up his mind. It would be at the Anse au Foulon, now called 'Wolfe's Cove.' This was on the north bank a little over two miles above Quebec and so named because fuller's earth, used by the bleachers and clothmakers, was found there. It was much nearer the city than the brigadiers

had at first suggested, but if successful a lodgement could lead on to a speedy decision, and Wolfe was growing impatient. The Foulon had the added advantages that troops could be reinforced by those from Point Lévis, and that signal communication with Saunders, who intended to make a series of feints against Beauport, would present no difficulties. These feints were to be thorough and convincing. Part of the scheme was for Cook of the *Pembroke* to lay buoys off the shoals, as if marking a course for boats. The French tried to cut them away, but were prevented from doing so by ships' fire.

The final reconnaissance took place on 10 September, when Wolfe assembled a party near the mouth of the Etchemin River which included Rear Admiral Holmes, Monckton, Townshend, Carleton, Mackellar, and a few others among whom were James Chads, under whose direction the boats were to be launched, and Captain Delaune, who with Colonel Howe, would lead the assault. Chads had been chosen by Saunders and Holmes as the best boat navigator in the fleet.

Quebec from Point Lévis

His own little ship, the *Vesuvius*, was not involved, being with the main fleet, and he was on detached duty. Wolfe knew him from his Rochefort days in the *Magnanime*, and although he misnamed him 'Shads' he must have been glad of the selection.

The party had disguised themselves in 'grenadier coats', but this did not deceive an alert French officer at Sillery, on the opposite bank, who watched through his telescope and reported. But as troops had already been landed higher up the south bank to relieve the congestion in the ships, and as Wolfe had stakes planted in the ground as if laying out a new camp, he was perhaps deceived as to the real purpose of the mission. Certainly his post was not reinforced.

There was a failure in communication between Wolfe and his brigadiers at or immediately after the reconnaissance. This did not extend to Holmes and Chads or even to Colonel Burton, to whom Wolfe sent a note giving him the necessary instructions about bringing his men over from Point Lévis, once a lodgement had been made. Wolfe evidently did not make it clear to his principal subordinates that the Anse au Foulon was to be the place, for on 12 September, on the very eve of the operation, all three brigadiers signed a note requesting 'as distinct orders as the nature of the thing will admit of, particularly to the place or places we are to attack.' Wolfe replied tartly, and not very reasonably in the circumstances: 'It is not a usual thing to point out in the publick orders the direct spot of an attack, nor for any inferior Officer not charged with a particular duty to ask instructions upon that point,' but he conveyed the news that the landing was to take place at 'the *Foulon* distant two miles, or two miles & a half from Quebec.' He added, in a few sentences which outline one of the most intricate boat operations ever attempted:

I have desired Mr. Holmes to send the Boats down so that we may arrive about half an hour before day, as you desired; to avoid the disorder of a night attack; & I shall be present myself, to give you all the aid in my power. The Officer's who are appointed to conduct the divisions of Boats, have been strictly enjoin'd to keep as much order & to act as silently as the nature of this serve will admit of, & Captain Shads will begin to land the men a little this side of the naked rock, which you must remember to have seen, within which (to the Eastward) the Enemy is posted.

It was small wonder that Holmes stated later that the whole prospect filled him with misgivings. He spoke of it as:

> . . . the most hazardous and difficult Task I was ever engaged in . . . for the distance of the landing Place; the impetuosity of the Tide; the darkness of the Night; and the great chance of exactly hitting the very Spot intended, without discovery or alarm, made the whole extremely difficult: and the failing in any part of my Disposition, as it might overset the General's Plan, would have brought upon me an imputation of being the Cause of the Miscarriage of the Attack.

Holmes's flag flew in the *Sutherland*, which had anchored, with her little squadron round her, about 16 miles above Quebec. The ships were on the south side of the river, between the village of St. Nicholas and Cap Rouge promontory on the north shore. Wolfe spent 12 September on board, making final arrangements and issuing detailed orders. One message which was read to the troops put the whole situation before tham about as well as it could have done.

> The Enemy's force is now divided, great Scarcity of Provisions now in their Camp, and universal discontent among the Canadians; the second Officer in command is gone to Montreal or St. Johns, which gives reason to think that General Amherst is advancing into the Colony: a vigorous blow struck by the Army at this juncture may determine the Fate of Canada.
>
> Our Troops below are in readiness to join us; all the light artillery and tools we embarked at the Point of Levi, and the Troops will land where the French seem least to expect it.
>
> The first Body that gets on shore is to march directly to the Enemy, and drive them from any little Post they may occupy; the Officers must be careful that the succeeding bodies do not, by any mistake, fire upon those who go before them.
>
> The Battalions must form on the Upper Ground with expedition, and be ready to charge whatever presents itself. When the Artillery and Troops are landed, a Corps will be left to secure the Landing-place, while the rest march on, and endeavour to bring the French and Canadians to a Battle.
>
> The Officers and men will remember what their Country expects from them, and what a Determined body of soldiers, inured to War, is capable of doing against weak French Battalions, mingled with a

disorderly Peasantry. The Soldiers must be attentive and obedient to their Officers, and Resolute in the execution of their Duty.

This Order indicated how much knowledge Wolfe had gained from deserters, such as the departure of de Lévis and the fact that he, as well as Bougainville, had been supplied with detachments which did indeed 'divide' Montcalm's resources.

The convoy which Chads was to conduct downstream consisted of thirty flat-bottomed boats, three long-boats, two smaller ships' boats and a schooner which had boldly made her way past Quebec, firing her small swivel-gun and trying to live up to her absurd name, *The Terror of France*. Wolfe had taken passage in this little vessel to make a reconnaissance or two of his own, requesting her captain to go close inshore, so that she came under pretty heavy fire at times.

Tensions on board the *Sutherland* the day before embarkation were typical of those which affect men under the strain of an impending assault. Nerves were taut, tempers short, and Wolfe himself was unguarded in some of his expressions. Such an atmosphere was incomparably conveyed by Shakespeare in the night scene round the camp fires on the eve of Agincourt. It was to repeat itself forty-two years later in the crowded cabins of the *Elephant* as Nelson made his last-minute dispositions for the attack on the Danish fleet and forts at Copenhagen.

The anonymous note-taker on Wolfe's staff who made such vitriolic remarks about certain leading characters, had a violent prejudice against the Navy, which even extended to Saunders, and indeed against anyone who even faintly opposed Wolfe, who was very much his hero. He records some most uninhibited remarks by the general, among them that after his final meeting with Monckton 'Mr. Wolfe said to his own Family that the Brigadiers had brought him up the River and now flinch'd: he did not hesitate to say that two of them were cowards and one a villain.' This was most unjust, except that Murray seems always to have been the main-spring of disaffection, so much so that Wolfe remarked that Townshend was never so difficult when separated from his colleague. The diarist also states that when Wolfe was away in *The Terror of France* 'Messrs Murray and Townshend came aboard the Admiral' (i.e. the

Sutherland) 'and behaved very seditiously in respect of Mr Wolfe.'

As for Chads, the same writer includes by far the fullest account of the natural doubts and difficulties put forward by this comparatively junior officer:

. . . which gave reason to suspect someone had tampered with him. The General told him he should have made his objections earlier, though should the disembarkation miscarry he would shelter him from any Blame, that all that could be done was to do his utmost: that if Captain Chads would write anything to testify that the miscarriage was G. Wolfe's and not Capt. Chads that he would sign it. Chads still persisting in his absurdity the General told him he could do no more than lay his head on the block to save Chads – then left the cabin.

Howe's Light Infantry were to occupy the first six boats, followed by others carrying the 28th Regiment, the 43rd Regiment, the 47th Regiment, the 58th Regiment and a party of Highlanders and Royal Americans. Captain Delaune was in the leading boat, and Wolfe himself in an early one. The total to be carried was 1,700. A further 1,900 were to follow later in the frigate *Lowestoft*, to which Holmes would transfer his flag, and in the *Squirrel, Seahorse, Hunter* and transports. In these ships would go the 15th Regiment, the Louisbourg Grenadiers, the 78th Regiment, more Light Infantry, the Royal Americans and the 35th Regiment. The *Hunter* was ordered down river, to anchor about $3\frac{3}{4}$ miles from the Foulon towards the south side. She would serve as a mark boat for Chads, who, assuming he had safely negotiated the first $10\frac{1}{4}$ mile leg, with a tide beneath him running at 6 knots and the river swollen by the recent rain, would need new bearings for the second, shorter and final one which would bring the convoy to the landing place.

It so happened that the French were also expecting to run a convoy that night down to Quebec with badly needed provisions. The barges had actually reached the mouth of the Cap Rouge River, not far from where the British ships were anchored, when it was discovered that they were leaking badly, and needed caulking before they could attempt the most hazardous part of their run. Under the circumstances the Intendant signified that he would have the journey made by

Men of the 60th Foot (left) and Rangers (right)

cart. Unfortunately for him and for others, the sentries on the north bank were not told of the alteration of plan. This had a most important effect on the success of the river passage, which presented so many hazards.

The night of the attempt was fine, calm and still, and as it was also dark, conditions for the concealment of dispositions were ideal. Such signs as were available suggested that good weather would continue next day. This was also fortunate for if, after all this time, Wolfe brought Montcalm to battle, the day would be decided by the musket. Rain had saved the assaulting grenadiers from complete annihilation on 31 July by soaking the French powder. It could have played havoc in the boats even before the landing: but for Wolfe, this was 'the lucky moment in war.'

The men were embarked about midnight. It was a cardinal point of deception that watchers on the north shore of the river should not merely be unaware of this, but should be able to assure themselves that the *Sutherland* herself remained where she was. The flag-ship did not, in fact, weigh anchor until daylight, and then made a leisurely passage down-stream.

The boat journey would take between two and three hours, and it was hoped that most of the troops would have landed not later than four o'clock in the morning. Chads waited for lanterns to be hoisted in the *Sutherland's* upper rigging as his signal to start, and then he slipped, the boats following in strict order, as arranged. The ship's lanterns remained in place, a visible proof to the French that the big ship continued to be where she had been the day before.

All went well. In these three words are contained the justification for meticulous planning at short notice, clear orders, strict discipline, silence, and rare skill on the part of Chads and the junior naval officers under his immediate command.

On the final leg of the journey the convoy was indeed challenged by sentries on the bank, and there are varied versions of what took place, some of them fanciful.

According to some, the following dialogue took place between shore and boats:

Sentry: Qui vive?
Reply: France!
Sentry: A quel regiment?

Reply: De la Reine.

The man who is said to have answered was Captain Donald McDonald of Fraser's Regiment, a reprieved Jacobite who had picked up a good accent serving abroad.

As the boats were passing the Samos Battery near Sillery, another French voice rang out. This time McDonald answered: *Convoi de vivres: ne fait pas de bruit, les Anglais nous entendraient!*

Townshend, who was in a fair position to know, jotted down a note on the challenge which in its quaint way has its interest, though as usual he was undramatic, and he gave credit to another for a ready response. Even so, it was a Highlander. The Brigadier wrote: '. . . when ye first corps for disembarkation was passing down ye N: Side of ye River & ye french Centries on ye bank's challeng'd our boats, Captn Frazer who had been in ye Dutch Service & spoke french – answered – la france & vive le Roy, on which ye French Centinels ran along ye Shore in ye dark crying laisser les passer its sont nos Gens avec les provisions. . . '

So much for that; and as the French had omitted to arrange a pass-word, there was no means other than direct question for the sentries to check the information. As the boats went past in the darkness, as fast as anyone on shore could run, they must have marvelled at what a formidable procession was making for the city. They would have been glad to think of so many boat loads with supplies, for this would mean that Quebec should fare better than it had done of late.

There was nearly a mishap, which could have been serious, due to temporary failure of recognition as Chads approached the mark-ship *Hunter*, for his boats could well have been French. Those on deck were about to open fire when the *Hunter's* captain, Adams, who knew by now from deserters that the enemy convoy had been cancelled, hastened to the ship's side to greet Chads with the assurance that all was quiet on the north shore, and likely to continue so.

Chads, who had by then achieved the most difficult part of his task, now had only the final leg before him. Considering the swiftness of the tide, the numbers and variety of the craft involved, to say nothing of having to operate in darkness throughout, it was a memorable feat, implying exact calculation, nerve and coolness. There have been many difficult and hazardous boat journeys since that time, made under stress of war, so that a far greater number will today be able to appreciate Chads at his true stature than was the case in the past.

He finished his task as he had begun it – superbly. Some of the leading boats headed inshore to beach a few hundred yards further downstream than had been planned, but this did not prove to be of any consequence. Most of them found the Anse au Foulon at once. It is hard not to over-praise such navigation in such circumstances.

Admiral Saunders, as is so often appropriate, may be given the last word on the subject, and as usual what he said was sober, exact, but lacking that touch of colour which, for once at least, the event could have justified. Remarking that both the boats and the follow-up by ship reached the Foulon 'just in the Time that had been concerted' (which was a triumph in itself) the admiral continued: 'Considering the Darkness of the Night, and the rapidity of the Current, this was a very critical Operation, and very properly and successfully conducted'*

II

The Cliffs rose about 175 feet above the Anse au Foulon. A transverse path, now a motor road, ascended from west to east. It was such that a French officer who had inspected it earlier in the summer reported that it was possible for two men to descend abreast. That it was good and usable is proved by the fact that guns were hauled up it; two that same morning, and others during the following days. Townshend later referred with admiration to the part the seamen played in this stiff work.

What exactly happened and where every unit landed in the darkness will never be known with accuracy, but what is certain is that some parties used the path and others scrambled up steeper

---

* Chad's reward came later, when Saunders was First Lord of the Admiralty. He was promoted, and ended his career as one of the Captains of Greenwich Hospital. Cook, who was given a similar appointment after his (second) circumnavigation of 1772–5, called the post a 'fine retreat, and a pretty income.' Both men had earned it, Cook by one of the longest journeys on record, Chads by a short one.

The taking of Quebec

places as best they could. Wolfe himself was at first pessimistic about whether or not it would be possible to get up at all. Saunders, writing his despatch only a week later, said:

When General Wolfe and the Troops with him had landed, the Difficulty of gaining the Top of the Hill is scarce credible. It was very steep in its Ascent and high, and had no Path where two could go a-breast; but they were obliged to pull themselves up by the Stumps and Boughs of Trees, that covered the Declivity.

This suggests that the regular path was used little at first, and that the exertions and enterprise of Howe, Delaune and Light Infantrymen who scrambled up anyhow and eliminated a post at the cliff-top held by Louis de Vergor, made things smooth for the rest. It enabled the hundreds assembled on the fore-shore, including those from the other side of the river who were ferried across as soon as boats were available, to use the better route. Even so, until all French outposts had been silenced, landing

Troops landing at the Anse au Foulon

parties were subject to fire. There was a four gun battery at
Samos, west of the Foulon, which opened up and did slight
damage to the frigates *Lowestoft* and *Seahorse*, while Captain
Knox of the 43rd Regiment, who was in the fifteenth boat,
reported eight casualties. Wolfe sent Murray to deal with the
threat, but soon recalled him. His mere advance made the French
spike their guns, and Light Infantry later got possession.

Surprise had been achieved; co-ordination between the Point
Lévis forces and those of the convoy had been excellent, and it
now remained for Wolfe to draw up his army in such a way as to
defeat Montcalm. A fugitive from de Vergor's post was on his
way to Quebec with news that the British had landed in strength,
and the troops at Beauport, who had stood to arms all night
watching the manoeuvres of the ships and boats in Quebec
Basin, had scarcely turned in before they were roused once
more, to face the real thing.

The light was growing, and Wolfe was given all the time he

needed. He was fairly between Montcalm and the French supply line, though he was himself between Montcalm and Bougainville. But recollecting the speed and secrecy of the boat journey, he disregarded the possibility of an attack from the rear, and his faith was justified, at least during the vital hours before the main clash of arms.

Bougainville has often been blamed for his passivity during the next few hours, but his chief fault seems to have been his failure to notify the upriver posts of the cancellation of the provision convoy. He was deceived by movements by Holmes's ships, or some of them, not long before the troops were embarked in their boats. These movements were made up-stream, and they had their effect, like those of Saunders before

Wolfe's last letter to Townshend

Landing & attack at the *Foulon*, if he succeeds, you will be pleas'd to give direc that the Troops afloat be set on shoar w the utmost expedition; as they are under yo command: and when the 3600 men w in the fleet are landed, I have no mean of doubt, but, that we are able to fight & to beat the French Army; in which I know you will give your best assistance

I have the honour to be

Sutherland
8 o'Clock.
12th Sept. 1759.

Sir
Your most Obed & most Humble Servant
Jam: Wolfe

Beauport, for Bougainville was at Cap Rouge largely for the purpose of guarding the provision barges, and it was on the cards that Wolfe would attack them, a matter for which Bougainville had to be fully prepared. It would have been a serious matter for Quebec if the provisions had been destroyed or captured, and Bougainville would have been blamed had this occurred. As it was, Bougainville observed that the big *Sutherland* stayed all night at her anchorage, he missed the slipping away of Chad's boat convoy, and he did not have news of Wolfe's landing, so he told Bourlamaque, until eight in the morning. Then he moved at once.

As his battalions reached the top of the cliff, Wolfe formed them in line, at first with their backs to the river, with Quebec to their right and St. Michel, where he had once, early on in the campaign, thought of attacking, to their left. Then, accompanied by his ADCs, who were his means of conveying orders, he made a reconnaissance towards the city to decide the best ground to take up. By eight o'clock, with the light excellent, Burton's men were over from Point Lévis, and the army was concentrated.

Wolfe needed open ground for deployment. This was in front of him, and was between him and Quebec, being part of the Heights or Plains of Abraham. It was ideal for his regulars, and it afforded them, with its contours, a certain amount of cover. The danger zones were on each flank. There, woods and shrub gave an opportunity for infiltration by Canadiens and Indians. It was exactly the sort of terrain to which they were best suited, and they lost no chance, from a very early hour, of harassing their enemies. Long before Montcalm's main advance, skirmishing was continuous, though it was never serious enough to hold up Wolfe's deployment.

By six o'clock, three battalions and the Louisbourg Grenadiers were in line, and they were put to face Quebec. As more units came up, the line was revised and extended until in the end it consisted, from right to left, of the 35th, which was on the flank facing the cliff, the Louisbourg Grenadiers, the 28th, 43rd, 47th, 78th (Highlanders), 58th, and then, on the left flank, the 15th and the Royal Americans. The Light Infantry were at grips with Canadian militia and Indians in the wooded area still further to the left, and a detachment of Royal Americans

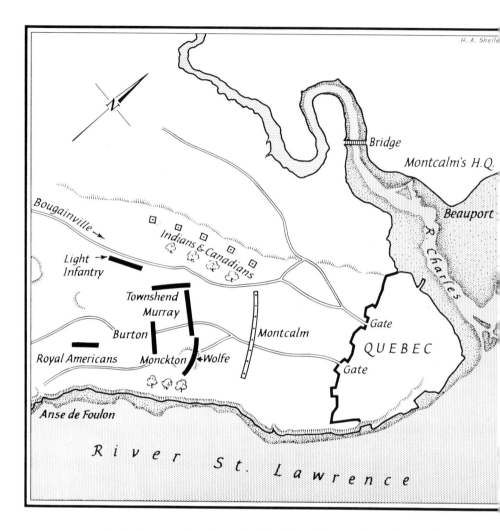

guarded the route back to the Foulon. The 48th, under Colonel Burton, formed a reserve and were placed behind Monckton, who had command of the right. Murray was in charge of the centre and Townshend of the left.

Wolfe posted himself at the head of the Louisbourg Grenadiers on the right flank, which, as the order of battle was finally drawn up, was slightly nearer Quebec than any other part of the line. He was also close at hand to direct Burton's reserve as necessary.

This was the array which stood to arms on that 13th day of September 1759, and which bequeathed the battle-honour 'Quebec' to regimental successors. The disposition was masterly and, once he had made certain that his men would be in the exact position he intended before the French could become aware of their strength, Wolfe had perfect control of them. Estimates of his numbers vary surprisingly. Townshend reckoned later that Wolfe had 4,400 men at his disposal, and he would be opposed on the battlefield by about the same number.

There were three cardinal elements in Wolfe's favour – his own serene confidence, which quickly spread to the troops; the training and spirit of his men, who were at long last at the stage for which they had made the weary journey to Canada, poised and ready; and the fact that, whatever last-minute moves the French might make, they must accept battle on his terms, not their own. The British were indeed so formed that if they maintained fire discipline, a matter to which Wolfe had given the strictest attention all his professional life, both on the field of battle and during the arduous months of training which preceded and followed action with the enemy, the result of the encounter now so close could be swift and decisive.

III

Whilst Wolfe was issuing his battle-orders undisturbed by opposition except on the flanks, Montcalm was in a very different situation. It was his custom, whenever he was at Beauport, to spend his time booted and spurred, whether by day or night.

Montbeillard, an artillery officer who kept the marquis's Journal posted for him, had an entry concerning the events of the night of 12/13 September which dealt mainly with the alarms in the Camp, the result of Saunders's activity. It was the continuation which was significant.

A little before day-break some musket shots were heard above Quebec. We had no doubt that a convoy of provisions we were expecting had been discovered and perhaps captured. By what fatal circumstances, when the city signalled, did no one send to find out what had happened, and why was the Regiment of Guienne, which it had been decided should camp on the Heights above Quebec, still in our Camp?

BASON

Low Water Mark

High

POINTE du PERES

ENCE

River Icherming

Contemporary map by des Barres, hitherto unpublished

It is clear that Montcalm's headquarters, like the sentries on the river bank, had not been told of the cancellation of the Cap Rouge convoy. But by dawn at the latest Montcalm, Montbeillard and the rest had gathered the worst. One of de Vergor's men, badly shaken, arrived at the St. Charles River with news that the British were forming up on the Heights of Abraham. The effect was stunning. In boxing terms, Montcalm faced a left and a right. The left, from the river, was a feint. The punch intended for annihilation would come from the right, from the direction he could least have expected.

Not much help could be looked for from the Governor General, who even at that early hour was already beginning to fuss.

At a quarter to seven Vaudreuil sent off a note to Bougainville enquiring whether the British had made any attempt against him, adding, in a very superfluous postscript: 'I do not doubt you will be attentive to enemy movements and follow them.' Long before the missive reached him, Bougainville had become aware of the situation, and was on the march to Quebec.

As for Montcalm, he rode across the St. Charles river on a black charger in a mood of shock and dejection. He had been utterly taken in by Saunders's bluff, by the din and firing and manoeuvring of ships and boats which had gone on all night, accompanied by signals, laying of buoys and markers, and everything pointing to an immediate attack upon Beauport. This had been intended to blind the French as to Wolfe's real objective and it had brilliantly succeeded. Montcalm had even reinforced his Beauport artillery. Now, in a flash, he saw how completely he had been out-generalled.

Montcalm was not only depressed, he had lost his usual cool decision. Wolfe, too, had his difficulties: he had arrived, but he was not yet master of all the ground in front of Quebec. He would have to fight hard for any success worth while, and a wily and experienced soldier such as Montcalm need not have despaired. Yet that is what he almost seems to have done. Major Malartic, of the Béarn battalion of French regulars, rode beside his chief as he made his way towards his opponent. As a rule, Montcalm was an animated talker: now he was silent. 'It seemed,' said Malartic, 'as though he felt his fate upon him.'

What worried Montcalm most was the quality of his men. Although in numbers the opposing forces were not unequal. Montcalm had less than 2,900 regulars available, and it was on their behaviour he had now to rely. Even before the battalions reached the Heights, their Canadien comrades-in-arms had shown how stubbornly they could fight on the perimeter. If the European-trained men could do as well, Wolfe, for all the advantage he had gained in surprise, might well be driven back in disorder to the river.

By half past nine, only a holding force remained at Beauport. The rest were facing, or about to face, the British, who did not advance to meet them. Wolfe was adopting, for the first time in the campaign, the role of the one who does the waiting.

Montcalm ranged his forces in the following order: on his right, flanked in the woods by Canadien militia and Indians under Dumas, was the regular contingent from Quebec and Montreal. Then came five attenuated French battalions: La Sarre: Languedoc: Béarn and Guienne in the centre: Royal Roussillon. On the left flank were men of Trois Rivières and Montreal; militia and Indians being spread out, somewhat ahead of them near the edge of the cliff. There were five guns, and there might have been more had the French been given time to organise: even so, this was three more than Wolfe's men had as yet been able to haul up the cliff.

Montbelliard, crossing the battlefield on one of his errands, had the chance to speak with Montcalm just before the general gave the word to advance. He wrote later:

I paused a moment with M. le Marquis de Montcalm, who said to me: 'We cannot avoid action. The enemy is entrenching. He already has two pieces of cannon. If we give him time to establish himself, we shall never be able to attack him successfully with the sort of troops we have.' He added, with a sort of shiver: 'Is it possible that Bougainville does not hear all that noise?' He left me without giving me time to say anything in reply, except that we were very thin on the ground.

At about ten o'clock, Montcalm gave the command, and the French advanced. The British were not entrenched, as Montcalm supposed. They were lying down, except for those actively engaged on the flanks, having been employed in making sure that their first volley, double shotted, was ready. That seen to, no doubt they consumed some of the two days' rations, and the rum, which they had taken with them into the boats. Wolfe placed his battalions in open order, with forty yard intervals between them, and as the line was extended, and many troops were needed to guard the flanks, the ranks were only two deep.

The French came on too fast – at a run, reported Major Malartic, who as a regimental officer would have noted such an important detail. The result was that the formations began to go to pieces almost at once, taking on a ragged appearance. 'We had not gone twenty paces,' said Malartic, 'before the left was too far in the rear, and the centre too far in front.' Worse even than that, the first French volley was fired too far from the British to be fully effective, and the second was feeble or non-existent, for the Canadian-born troops who reinforced the French battalions, 'according to their custom, threw themselves on the ground to re-load.' When they rose, it was not to fire again, but to retreat. They had no stomach for the sort of fighting, volleys followed up by an assault with the bayonet, for which the regulars had been drilled. The scarlet-coated British and the white-coated French were now in direct contact, but as yet, no firing had come from Wolfe's ranks.

Brown Bess (the name derived from *bus*, the Dutch for a gun) had yet to speak, but was ready. The complex sequence of orders: 'Handle Cartridge' – draw the cartridge from the pouch and bite the top off – 'Prime' – shake the powder into the priming pan – 'Load' – put the ball and wadding into the barrel – 'Draw ramrods' – press down with ramrod and withdraw – 'Return ramrods' – return to loop on the musket and fix bayonet – 'Make ready' – face to the front – 'Present' – had already been given.

Only the order '*Give Fire*' was reserved until the last second. Wolfe's entire experience of battle had shown the value of withholding fire until the enemy was deadly close: at Quebec, the distance was forty yards. Then at last, when the final bark of command came, the result blasted the French battalions from from the field. Only a single volley was necessary. There would be no immediate re-loading. The rest of the grim work would fall to bayonets, or, in the case of the Highlanders, claymores.

Sir John Fortescue, historian of the British Army, spoke of this volley as the most perfect ever fired on a battlefield, and it was decisive. It was not quite instantaneous, except in the centre, where it seems to have been delivered like a single cannon shot, but it was near enough. The climax came within seconds, not minutes, and, as a regular formation, Montcalm's army broke and fled. In those seconds, Wolfe had the fullest justification for years of rigorous discipline and training. The volley was among the last sounds he heard coherently.

He had exposed himself recklessly throughout the French advance, and within minutes he was thrice wounded. The first time it was his right wrist, which he bound up with a handkerchief. The second shot was in the groin, but probably from a spent bullet, since he was still able to move about freely. The third was in the chest. According to Townshend's despatch, it did not come until after the famous volley, for the words were: 'our General fell at the head of Braggs (the 35th) and the Louisbourg Grenadiers advancing with their Bayonets.' Whether it was a chance shot, or was aimed deliberately, as one story related, by a deserter, it was likely to have come from a marksman on the edge of the cliff above the St. Lawrence.

Captain John Knox of Kennedy's Regiment the 43rd, a seasoned campaigner who set down with great care his version of all the more notable episodes of the expedition, was at pains to collect information about Wolfe's last moments. His account runs as follows:

... he desired those who were about him to lay him down; being asked if he would have a Surgeon he replied, 'it is needless; it is all over with me.' One of them cried out, 'they run, see how they run.' 'Who runs?' demanded our hero, with great earnestness, like a person roused from sleep. The Officer answered, 'The enemy, Sir; Egad, they give way everywhere.' Thereupon the General rejoined, '*Go one of you, my lads, to Colonel Burton – tell him to march Webb's regiment with all speed to Charles's River, to cut off the retreat of the fugitives from the bridge.*' Then turning on his side he added, '*Now, God be praised, I will die in peace:*' and thus expired.

This version rings true since Wolfe, having won his battle, would not have been content with anything less than a thoroughgoing follow-through. The account of his last moments left by the unknown staff-officer who made such cogent notes on

certain personalities adds a highly significant detail: 'As they
carried him off, he wav'd his hat to Otway's regiment to move
up and flank the Enemy.' These last gestures, which would have
been obeyed at once had Wolfe lived, showed how set he was
upon completing his victory. He had seen the important
business of pursuit neglected far too often on other battle-fields.

Burton's reserve, Webb's 48th Regiment, drawn up behind
Monckton to exploit any success or to retrieve any reverse,
would have been put to the best use. Wolfe also saw that if
Otway's, the 35th, advanced as quickly as possible on the right,
the French would be driven in the direction he intended, and
crushed as they tried to make their way across the St. Charles
to Beauport.

The two people nearest to Wolfe when he was mortally
wounded were Lieutenant Henry Browne and Volunteer James
Henderson, both of the Louisbourg Grenadiers. Unknown to
Captain Knox, Henderson wrote an account of his experiences
to a relation in England. His letter survives, heavily creased and
stained as the result of many unfoldings.

Our Company of Grenadiers was the Right of the Line, (he wrote).
Upon the General viewing the Position of the two Armies, he took
notice of a small rising ground between our Right and our Enemy's
Left who concealed their Motions from View . . . upon which the
Genl. did me the honour to Detach me with a few Grenadiers to take
Possession and Maintain it to the last extremity which I did.

And then the Genl. came to me and took his Post by me. But Oh!
how can I tell, my dear Sir. Tears flow from my eyes still as I write.
That Great, ever memorable Man whose loss can never be enough
Regretted was scarce a moment with me till he received his fatal
Wound. I myself received at the same time a Wound, for I was close
to him, in the Right Shoulder and one in the Thigh. But my concern
for Him was so great that I did not at the time think of them.

When the Genl. received the Shot I caught hold of him and Carried
him off the Field – he walked about one Hundred Yards and then
beg'd I would set him down which I did. Then I open'd his Breast and
found his Shirt full of blood at which he smiled and when he seen the
distress I was in, 'My Dear,' said he, 'Don't grieve for me I shall be
happy in a few Minutes take care of Yourself as I see you are Wounded.
But tell me O tell me how goes the Battle?'

Just then came some Officers who told him that the French had

Penney's version of Wolfe's death

given Ground and that our Troups was pursuing them to the Walls of the Town. He was then Lying in my arms just Expiring. That great Man whose sole Ambition was his Country's Glory raised Himself upon the News and Smiled in my Face. 'Now' said he 'I die Contented' – from that Instant the Smile never left his Face till he Deided. ★

★ Nothing shows Monckton in a better light than what followed. Although himself wounded almost at the same moment as Wolfe, and carried to the *Lowestoft*, no sooner was the immediate fighting over than the Brigadier sent for Henderson and gave him then and there an Ensign's commission in the 28th Regiment. Henderson was made a lieutenant three years later.

IV

With Wolfe dead and Monckton off the field, with the British advancing in the centre and the French everywhere retreating pell mell, the Heights of Abraham were transformed, within a few minutes, from a scene of orderly troop disposition to one of scurry and confusion. For a time at least, no one was in supreme control on either side.

British casualties were only 58 killed as against 600 wounded, but as the dead included Wolfe, and the wounded not only Monckton, but Carleton and Barré, it was no great wonder that Townshend, finding himself in charge, took some time to appreciate the tactical situation. Most of the regiments were in hard, somewhat disorderly pursuit of the French, Saunders giving the detail in his despatch that 'our Troops pursued quite to the Walls, and killed many upon the Glacis and in the Ditch; and if the Town had been further off, the whole French Army must have been destroyed.'

Montcalm had been seriously wounded and his second in command, Brigadier Senezeagues, was a prisoner in British hands. He had not long to live, for he had been worse hit than Monckton. Montcalm's wound was in the stomach. It had probably been caused by grape-shot from one of Colonel Williamson's two brass 6-pounders, for he had been a conspicuous target as he rode, drawn sword in hand, urging on his infantry. He was borne back by a crowd of fugitives through the St. Louis gate of Quebec, where a group of women replaced the escort of soldiers which had been supporting him in the saddle. 'O mon Dieu,' they cried, 'le marquis est tué!' 'Ce ne'est rien,' answered the general, 'ne vous afflgez pas pour moi, mas bonnes amies.'

It was the French centre which retreated furthest and fastest. The Canadians on Townshend's original front continued to resist stubbornly, and never joined the rout of the French regulars, whose breaking they were not to forget. They could operate at least partly behind cover, and very skillfully they did so, hopeful no doubt of the arrival of Bougainville and, with his advent, of a reversal of fortune. So far, it all seemed too bad to be true.

Bougainville came – he could scarcely have done otherwise – but too late. Like Montcalm, he had been out-generalled, and by the time he had hastened, horse and foot, from his watching position upstream towards the ominous and unexpected sound of battle, Townshend, who had by now assumed control of what were much scattered British units, was able to face him with Burton's reserve. To this was added another battalion which he was able to recall from the pursuit by means of an ADC.

In his official despatch, Townshend refers to Bougainville's arrival.

This, Sir, (he wrote) was the situation of things when I was told, in the Action, that I commanded: I immediately repaired to the Centre, and finding the Pursuit had put part of the Troops in Disorder, I formed them as soon as possible. Scarce was this effected, when Mr Bougainville, with his corps from Cape Rouge, of 2,000 men, appeared in our Rear. I advanced two Pieces of Artillery, and two Battalions towards him; upon which he retired. You will not, I flatter myself, blame me for not quitting such advantageous Ground, and risking the Fate of so decisive a Day, by seeking a fresh Enemy, posted perhaps in the very kind of Ground he could wish for, viz: Woods and Swamps.

As the day wore on, Townshend found himself in a situation not without perplexities. His army was between a beaten opponent, and another, unbeaten, who had retreated, but whose force included cavalry, of which he had none. The city lay before him, as yet unassailed, and there had been no time to probe its weaknesses when approached by land. Morally, he was in the ascendant, and his communications with river and fleet were as secure as he and the sailors could make them. But it was very soon apparent that the British army before Quebec under Wolfe and under Townshend were two different instruments.

Ever since his landing, Wolfe had shown complete tactical mastery, and with his dying breath he indicated how completely he would have continued. Townshend's first idea seems to have been to get as many guns up the hill as he could – Knox says he had no less than 60, in addition to 58 howitzers and mortars, within a few days – and to set about a formal siege of the city, just as if it had been one of those Continental fortresses against which he had served a military apprenticeship. That he did not meet with an early reverse was due as much to luck as to skill, and to the fact that the enemy were demoralised, at least for the time. 'He is without scale,' commented the notetaker on Wolfe's staff, about Townshend's military capabilities. He put the matter shrewdly.

Meanwhile Vaudreuil, who Montcalm so often and so ironically referred to as the 'Generalissimo', had not been early on the scene of encounter, and he did not linger long in the neighbourhood. The Governor General made his way to Beauport, as being the right place for the King's Representative. There was no point whatever in his risking capture.

Yet now that Vaudreuil found himself in fact what he had so long believed that he should be, the undisputed military commander, he felt the need of Montcalm's advice as never before. He sent a message from Beauport to the general whose condition was deteriorating, asking what course he would favour next.

Montcalm saw three alternatives, if the message he sent by Martel, his ADC, was accurately delivered. The first was capitulation 'for the whole Colony', which seemed a needlessly pessimistic notion seeing that he and the Governor General had already gained yet another campaigning season for France, by the defence they had already put up. The second was to launch a new attack there and then. Of its prospect of success Montcalm could be no judge from his bed of pain. Routed troops rarely counter-attack successfully unless wonderfully well led, and who would lead them? The third was a retirement on the Jacques Cartier River, where Vaudreuil could no doubt join forces not only with Bougainville, but with de Lévis if that capable man were to be summoned with all speed.

Vaudreuil called a Council of War, at which Bigot the Intendant and surviving senior officers were present. It met early in the evening, and it was over by six o'clock. The decision was in favour of a retreat up the east bank of the St. Charles, the idea being to march round the British position, if they would allow this. There was considerable fear that they would not: it would have been unthinkable to Wolfe, but Townshend had no

Ruin of the Bishop's House

strong detachments out which might have prevented them, and by nine o'clock, under cover of darkness, the army was away on what Malartic described as 'a forced march, with little order', in fact, conducted in precipitate haste, artillery, ammunition and supplies being left behind for want of transport. The escape, for this is how the movement was thought of, rather than a formal retreat, was made without interference, to Vaudreuil's huge relief.

The garrison remaining inside Quebec was a small one, and had very little powder left for the guns. Moreover, few houses were habitable, so knocked about they had been in the British bombardments.

V

The next day, September 14th, started badly for the French garrison at Quebec. At four o'clock in the morning Montcalm died, under the care of the Ursulines, exactly a day after Wolfe had landed at the Anse au Foulon. He was buried almost at once in the convent chapel in a bomb-crater which had been made by a projectile fired from Point Lévis.

The event inspired many expressions of sorrow within the city, and (as soon as they heard of it, for they were in full flight at the time), from the ranks of the French regulars, who had served their leader in success as well as in set-back. If it had produced a tribute from Vaudreuil, such a gesture would have warmed many hearts; but the Governor General's dislike followed Montcalm beyond the grave. When, in due course Vaudreuil sat down to write his official report on the leading events of the campaign, he included many pages of vituperation. His summary was that:

from the moment of M. de Montcalm's arrival in this Colony, down to that of his death, he did not cease to sacrifice everything to his boundless ambition. He sowed dissention among the troops, tolerated the most improper talk against the Government, and attached to himself the most disreputable persons. He used means to corrupt the most virtuous, and when he could not succeed, became their implacable enemy. Above all, he wanted to be Governor General. (He

The death of Montcalm

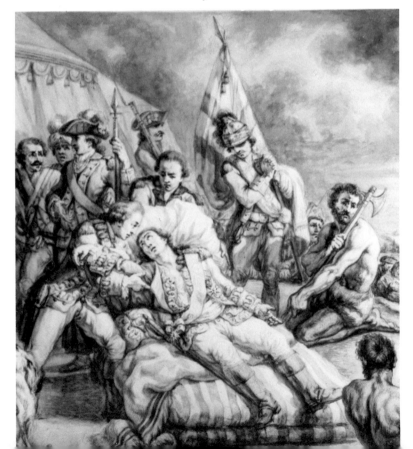

concluded): If I had been sole master, Quebec would still belong to the King.

Even if what Vaudreuil said had been entirely true, it would have been best forgotten in the misfortunes which beset New France. The generous note was utterly lacking, and if one thing is more certain than another, it is that Quebec would have not held out longer had the Governor General been in sole charge.

On the following day, 15 September, the Chevalier de Ramezay who was now in charge at Quebec summoned the senior officers of his garrison. He pointed out that although the city might resist for some time longer, if properly provisioned, food stores were so low that the meagre existing ration would soon have to be reduced, and at best could only last a few days without replenishment. There were fourteen present besides himself, and he asked everyone to give their views in writing. All but one advised capitulation, chiefly on the grounds of shortages. The exception was a veteran gunner captain, de Fiedmont, who voted to 'reduce the ration again, and persevere in defending the place to the last extremity.'

There is often at least one de Fiedmont even in the more pusillanimous Councils of War, but such stout spirits do not always prevail. It was so in this instance. Vaudreuil had left instructions with de Ramezay to the effect that he was not to try to hold out until the city was taken by assault, 'thus, as soon as food runs short, he will hoist the white flag.' Pressed by the leading citizens to treat for terms, he agreed to do so.

On the same day Vaudreuil made contact with Bougainville, whose first thought was to communicate with de Ramezay, urging him to hold out until the two of them, with de Lévis, who was hurrying from Montreal, could make a concerted effort to relieve the city. Among Bougainville's officers was an enterprising cavalryman, Captain de la Rochebeaucourt, able and willing to lead a reconnaissance back to Quebec.

The situation for Vaudreuil was by no means without possibilities. For two days later, when de Lévis took over effective command of the army, on 17 September, Bougainville, with his elite troops, was within a mile or two of Townshend's camp as the spear-head of a fresh advance.

But moves by Saunders during these two days now brought

matters to a head. 'Immediately after our Victory over their troops,' wrote the admiral, 'I sent up all the Boats in the Fleet with Artillery and Ammunition; and on the 17th went up with the Men of War, in a Disposition to attack the Lower Town, but in the evening they sent out to the Camp, and offered terms of Capitulation.'

Later that night de la Rochebeaucourt successfully rode round the British lines and actually established a troop, for a time at least, at the crossing over the St. Charles River. This was an episode which Wolfe would never have allowed to occur; he would have been far too alert.

de Ramezay had to tell the captain he was too late. The British had agreed to the terms proposed, except for a proviso which would have allowed the garrison to march out to join de Lévis's army. That was indeed asking much. The Governor had sent his Town Major back to Townshend and Saunders with full powers to clinch the matter. He added, however, that if any article was refused, he should break off the negotiations. No hitch occurred, and the Capitulation was signed in the British camp on the morning of 18 September.

The garrison was allowed the honours of war, and was to be 'embarked as conveniently as possible, to be sent to the first port in France.' Local property was to be respected and protected. The 'free exercise of the Roman religion' was guaranteed, and special safeguards were accorded to the clergy and particularly to the Bishop of Quebec. de Ramezay was much abused in France, and Vaudreuil told him, with typical spite, that he could explain matters personally to the Court of Versailles.

VI

The final military gestures were made in the surrendered city on the evening of 18 September. Fifty men of the Royal Artillery marched in, pulling a field-piece, with the British colours on its carriage. Colonel Williamson, the chief gunner, was given the honour of hoisting the victorious flag on the walls. The cannon was followed by the Louisbourg Grenadiers. They had been originally drawn from the grenadier companies of the

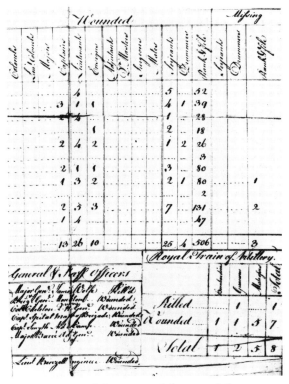

Part of the return of the wounded

22nd, 40th and 45th Regiments, and they were shortly to return to their own units. But they had long since developed a strong corporate spirit, and it was proper that they should have been chosen for the first guard-mounting ceremony at the city gates. Simultaneously with the hoisting of the flag, Captain Palliser of the Navy landed in the Lower Town with a body of seamen.

They had work to do, for Saunders's final duty was to provision the garrison from his ships, to help it to withstand the ardours and endurances of the cold months ahead. He was generous with what he spared, even to the extent of leaving himself short. Landing stores and tidying up in the Isle of Orleans and at Point Lévis took a month, and by 18 October the Admiral was ready to drop down the river, the last big ships weighing anchor a week later. Remembering the misadventures of the spring, Saunders stationed a strong detachment under Lord Colville at Halifax, with orders to re-enter the St. Lawrence at the first opportunity.

The garrison would have been sad to see the ships go, for it had been their constant presence, and the munitionment they were always able to supply, that had given the troops a sense that they were in every way backed up, and that if things came to the worst, they had a secure line of retreat.

As for Saunders, his common sense, experience and sheer authority had long been a source of strength to the brigadiers, as also, perhaps, to Wolfe, though it had only been in his gesture of leaving the admiral his silver plate that he had had an opportunity of showing it. But the fact that Saunders was a Vice-Admiral, while Wolfe was a local and temporary general officer, gave Saunders, although entirely independent, a position which could not be questioned. His views on military subjects, however tentatively expressed, could be listened to with respect.

The admiral sent news home of Wolfe's success within a very few days of the occupation of Quebec. It is not the hardest task in the world to compose a brief despatch full of surprisingly good news, and the official naval and military accounts were signed respectively by Saunders and Townshend on 20 September. Saunders thereupon ordered the *Alcide*, Captain James Douglas, to sail at once for England. The military officer sent with him was Lieutenant Colonel John Hale, of the 47th Regiment, which had been in the centre of the great day. Hale was Monckton's choice, but it was one which was approved by Townshend and Murray.

The *Alcide* made a fast passage, and was in Channel waters in less than a month. The news was given to the country in *The Public Advertiser* dated Friday 19 October, which was good going by the standards of the time. It was prefaced by a note from Monckton referring to 'the very signal Victory over the French' and stating the reason which prevented him, as senior surviving officer, from writing the despatch himself.

General Wolfe, (so he explained) exerting himself on the Right of our Line, received a Wound pretty early, of which he died soon after; and I myself had the great Misfortune of receiving one in my Right Breast by a Ball, that went through part of my Lungs (and which has been cut out under the Blade Bone of my Shoulder) just as the French were giving way; which obliged me to quit the Field.

John Hale

Feeling, perhaps, that he had said either too much or too little, Monckton added postscripts. The first stated: 'His Majesty's Troops behaved with the greatest Steadiness and Bravery.' The second was to re-assure his own well-wishers. 'As the Surgeons tell me there is no danger in my Wound, I am in Hopes that I shall soon be able to join the Army before the Town.' These hopes were realised.

Saunders paid tribute to the unity between the two Services which had continued throughout, at least so far as outward appearances were concerned, and there is no evidence that Wolfe's private complaints were at all widely shared.

During this tedious Campaign, (said the Admiral) there has continued a perfect good Understanding between Army and Navy. I have received great Assistance from Admirals Durell and Holmes, and from all the Captains; indeed, every Body has exerted themselves in the Execution of their Duty; even the Transports have willingly assisted me with Boats and People on the Landing the Troops, and many other Services.

Townshend, for his part, referred to the work of the Navy in a thoroughly handsome way. No one could have bettered the tribute.

I should not do Justice to the Admirals and the Naval Service, (he wrote) if I neglected this Occasion of acknowledging how much we are indebted for our Success to the constant Assistance and support received from them, and the perfect Harmony and Correspondence which has prevailed throughout all our Operations, in the uncommon Difficulties, which the Nature of this Country, in particular, presents to Military Operations of a great Extent, and which no Army can itself solely supply; the immense Labour in Artillery, Stores and Provisions, the long Watching and Attendance in Boats; the drawing up our Artillery by the Seamen, even in the Heat of Action: it is my Duty, short as my Command has been, to acknowledge, for that Time, how great a Share the Navy has had in this successful Campaign.

Only one ingredient was absent – any sort of valediction, even of the most conventional sort, directed to the memory of the dead leader. There was nothing whatever corresponding to the noble tribute which, for instance, Collingwood was to pay to Nelson after Trafalgar, such as moved the whole nation to admiration, and which caused even the garrulous George III to pause in respectful silence.

The omission seemed so odd and glaring that at the bottom of the third sheet of the newspaper some unknown scribe contributed the first of a thousand panegyrics, most of them trite and some of them excruciating, but all heart-felt.

To the PRINTER

Give me leave to offer the following Lines to the Memory of my glorious Friend.

Underneath, a Hero lies
WOLFE the Young, the Brave, the Wise:
No Tomb stone need his Worth proclaim
Quebec for ever shall record his Fame:
Quebec for ever shall with Wonder tell
How great, beneath her Walls, her Conqueror fell.

This was the beginning of Wolfe's apotheosis. It was to take strange forms, and was to continue for a long time.

PART FIVE
APOTHEOSIS

Burial at Greenwich
Wolfe's Reputation and Memorials

VIVERE MEMORIA FORTIS

APOTHEOSIS

I

SAUNDERS had sent the *Neptune* home early, choosing to return to England with his blue flag on the fore-top-masthead of the *Somerset*, 74 guns, Captain Edward Hughes. The captain was to win a reputation not many years later for a series of stubborn actions in Far Eastern waters against the greatest of all French naval tacticians, Suffren.

With that unerring sense of what was fitting which never seems to have failed him, Saunders chose the *Royal William* in which to convey Wolfe home. It was unthinkable that the nation should not wish to pay the general the respect of a public funeral, and his body was embalmed before being placed on board. The *Royal William*, if only by reason of her size – she was a three-decked ship – was unlikely to be attacked on her way back to England, so healthy a regard had the French for the largest rates of British ships of the line. In the handier *Somerset* Saunders would be able to cope with any emergency.

It so happened that the *Royal William* had the longest continuous history of any ship of war in the annals of the Navy. She had been built in 1670, during the reign of Charles II, as the *Prince*, and as such had earned two battle honours in the stern old maritime wars with the Dutch. She had been re-named *Royal William* in 1692, soon after what was known as the Glorious Revolution had brought William of Orange to the throne of Britain, and she had served at Barfleur, which ensured that he would stay there. She was present with Boscawen at Louisbourg in 1758, and although Quebec was to be her last battle honour, she was not broken up until 1813, after nearly a century and a half afloat.

The *Royal William* went on her stately way ahead of Saunders, and she arrived at Spithead on 16 November. The admiral himself had an encounter in the *Somerset* which could have led to his taking part in Sir Edward Hawke's victory over Conflans, Handelian in sweep and grandeur, among the rocks and shoals of Quiberon Bay.

On 18 November the flagship was approaching the entrance to the Channel when she was seen by the frigate *Juno*. The captain, Phillips, reported that the French were out in strength, and that Hawke, who had been driven back to Torbay by contrary winds, had just sailed out again in search of the enemy fleet. Townshend, who was Saunders's guest on board, described the effect of the news in a letter to his wife written the same day. 'The *Juno*,' he explained, had 'brought the Admiral dispatches by which I find that we are going this instant to join Sir Edward Hawke in search of the French fleet, supposed at Quiberon.'

But while holding on for the enemy coast, Saunders learnt that all was over with Conflans, and he informed his captains accordingly. The final touch had now been added to what, for the British nation, was to be known as 'The Wonderful Year.' Even the weather smiled. 'It is still all gold,' wrote Horace Walpole in the autumn. 'Instead of the Glorious and ever Memorable year of 1759, as the Newspapers call it, I call it this Ever-warm and Victorious year. We have not had more conquest than fine weather: one would think we had plundered the East and West Indies of sunshine.'

There was one officer, other than Saunders, likely to have been sorely disappointed at not having been at Quiberon on 20 November. This was Captain Augustus Hervey of the *Monmouth*. He had worn out himself, his men and his ship keeping the sea week after week as an outpost of Hawke's fleet, and done magnificently. He had then to be sent home a fortnight before the battle. There he found a long letter from his mother in which she described, among many lesser matters, the immediate effect of the news from Canada.

The King told Mr Pitt publicly at his levée (wrote Lady Hervey), the day the news came of taking Quebec: 'All your plans have succeeded.' Quebec is certainly a great acquisition, but 'tis gold bought too dear. Woolfe is an irreparable loss, such an head, such an heart, such a temper and such an arm are not easily to be found again.

He was an excellent scholar, knew all the advantages of the Roman

'Conquests of the Glorious 1759'

Phalanx and Grecian Discipline, had a memory that made all the past present to him, and he could therefore profit by all the battles fought and the sieges laid either by ancients or moderns: with all these public virtues he had also all the private ones, was the most tender, most dutiful son in the world and the most humane benevolent master: he has left a young lady to whom he was to have been married at his return inconsolable – 'tis a sister of Sir James Lowther's. His poor mother does

not feel the loss, she has been insensible since she heard the certain news
of his death – but what must that first feeling have been, to have worked
such an effect so immediately, poor, poor, miserable woman. I pity
her from my soul.

Lady Hervey had the right of it in her *feeling* for the victor of
Quebec, despite the over-bright colours of the character she
gave him. It was universal. Military paragons, the Marlboroughs
and the Wellingtons, compel admiration. Imperfect creatures,
the Wolfes and the Nelsons, win hearts, and never more fully
than when they die young.

The nation needed a new military hero, and if Wolfe had
been far less distinguished, the circumstances of his campaign,
and his death at the moment of victory would have elevated him
accordingly. He had no rival. Cumberland was certainly not
such, and neither were Ligonier nor the patient, sure-footed
Amherst. Clive, in India, was too far away. Wolfe's scope, it is
true, had been modest, but nothing warms like success,
particularly if it comes at exactly the right time. There was
also the fact that in Montcalm he had had a worthy opponent,
one who had gained precious months for his country when time
was of importance, and one who had behaved with chivalry.

Wolfe had seen himself with quite remarkable clarity – seen,
moreover, how little he had to fear from comparison with the
leaders of his own profession, in which there was, at the time,
no one of British blood to be mentioned in the same breath as
the nation's ally, Frederick the Great. The Prussian had grave
defects as a man, but as a soldier he stands high.

I reckon it a very great misfortune to this Country, (Wolfe had written
to his mother, before he had had the chance to exercise his gifts on any
extended scale) that I, your son, who have, I know, but a very modest
capacity, and some degree of diligence a little above the ordinary run,
should be thought, as I generally am, one of the best officers of my
rank in the Service. I am not at all vain of the distinction. The comparison would do a man of genius very little honour, and does not
illustrate me, by any means; and the consequence will be very fatal to
me in the end, for as I rise in rank people will expect some considerable
performance, and I shall be induced, in support of an ill-got reputation,
to be lavish of my life, and shall probably meet that fate which is the
ordinary effect of such conduct.

Henrietta Wolfe carefully preserved that letter, and it is well that she did so, for it adds much to the understanding of her son, and as self-analysis it is remarkable.

What of the side of the general seen by Townshend? The 'Honourable Brigadier', as a pamphleteer soon described him, with a touch of his own malice, was anything but a fool, but, as his later career was to show, he much preferred politics to soldiering, and even the most wary politicians are capable of outrageous blunders. By his omission of any public expression of sorrow for the loss of Wolfe, which was keenly felt by the rank and file of the Army who had won the battle for him, he had laid himself open to grave charges. They came thick and fast. He was accused of ingratitude, and of taking the first opportunity of returning home, as indeed he had always intended, having had Amherst's leave to do so when the immediate campaign was over – leaving his superior, Monckton, convalescent though acquiescing. The public might well wonder, and Townshend was, in fact, riding his luck.

His venomous cartoons – to which he added even after Wolfe's death – were circulating privately in England and abroad, yet in the end, after the manner of his kind, he got away with it – and at least he was not a hypocrite. People in general soon became too interested in more satisfactory matters, and in *commemorating* Wolfe, to allow of any prolonged attention to the state of mind of the third in command. Had Townshend wished to increase Wolfe's fame, instead of to diminish it, he could scarcely have set about it a better way, for he had given Wolfe's admirers a sense of grievance they were quick to exploit. Meanwhile, there was an oration in the general's praise which was held to be one of Pitt's less felicitous performances, and Townshend and the rest duly received the official Thanks of Parliament. Time healed many wounds. Forty years later, most survivors of Quebec remained firm friends. For instance John Jervis, by then the Earl of St. Vincent and a renowned admiral, was devoted both to Isaac Barré, a favourite with Wolfe, and to Townshend, who was not.

From the outset, interest in obtaining a good representation of Wolfe was considerable, and it was sponsored in high quarters. Charles Lennox, third Duke of Richmond and Lennox, led the

Wolfe's monument in Westminster Abbey

way. He was a great grandson of Charles II and Louise de Keroualle, Duchess of Portsmouth, a soldier, and an art patron of sufficient enthusiasm to have established a gallery at Whitehall, of which the directors were Joseph Wilton the sculptor and Giovanni Cipriani, historical painter and engraver.

The Duke had a special interest in Wolfe, for in June 1753 he had himself been gazetted captain in the 20th Regiment, of which Wolfe was at that time the lieutenant-colonel. A few weeks before Wolfe's death the Duke had distinguished himself under Prince Ferdinand of Brunswick's command at Minden, another contribution by the Army to the Wonderful Year.

According to Horace Walpole, who was always well-informed in art matters, the Duke: 'had a mind to have a statue of General Wolfe. Wilton the statuary went down to Portsmouth and opened his coffin when it was brought over, to try to take his face, but it was too much distorted. They found out a servant of Lord Gower, who was like Wolfe, and Wilton was ordered to model his face, and Lord Edgcombe was to correct it from memory.'

A glimpse of the coffined Wolfe would at least have given Wilton an idea of the shape of the general's head, which would have been useful to him when in course of time he was asked to design the Abbey monument. Meanwhile the coffin was taken with all due ceremony to Blackheath, and on 20 November, the day of Hawke's victory, it was buried at St. Alphege, Greenwich, beside that of his father. Today the church, which had been rebuilt in 1718 in the classical style by Nicholas Hawksmoor, is often locked against hooligans, but Wolfe's statue by Tait McKenzie has stood four square to the winds in Greenwich Park on the hill near the Observatory since it was unveiled in 1930 by the Marquis of Montcalm. From it can be enjoyed one of the finest panoramas in south London, and the white plinth, pitted by bomb blast, is a sharp reminder of how violence has continued.

Westerham, Wolfe's birth-place, did not forget him, and Quebec House, where he once lived, has long formed part of his memorial. In the Westerham church an epitaph was chiselled on a monument which suggests true feeling, and which might well have been composed by a member of the Warde family,

Quebec commemoration medal

the general's friends.

> Whilst George in sorrow bows his laurell'd head
> And bids the Artist grace the Soldier dead,
> We raise no sculptured trophy to thy name
> Brave youth! the fairest in the list of fame:
> Proud of thy birth, we boast th'auspicious year,
> Struck with thy fall, we shed a general tear;
> With humble grief inscribe one artless stone,
> And from thy matchless honours date our own.

Wolfe, in this matter like Nelson, cared very little for money. This was just as well, for he left no great fortune, and nothing was done for his mother out of the public funds – indeed, she could not even secure from the War Office what she believed to be her son's due. It did not greatly signify, for she had just means enough, at the time of her death in 1764, to discharge the general's legacies in full, and she had no other children then surviving.

What Wolfe cared most about he made plain to his parents and other close confidants. It was personal honour, expressed by conduct in battle. This will seem stranger today than it would have appeared in his own harder, narrower times. Today, there are far more opportunities for testing manhood by personal adventure than could have been known to a man with Wolfe's background: sailing, mountaineering, caving, parachuting, flying, above all perhaps the adventure of altruism – that of fostering or saving life instead of taking it. Centuries of suffering have increasingly sickened civilised man with warfare. Wolfe knew no such disgust, and this was not from any lack of direct experience.

A good illustration of the contemporary attitude may be found in Samuel Johnson, an otherwise unsoldierly character. The subject of one of the finest passages Johnson ever wrote, in his poem 'The Vanity of Human Wishes', was Charles XII of Sweden, a military portent whose exploits were familiar to Wolfe, as to every student of war of his time.

> A frame of adamant, a soul of fire,
> No dangers fright him, and no labours tire;
> O'er love, o'er fear, extends his wide domain,
> Unconquer'd lord of pleasure and of pain;
> No joys to him pacific sceptres yield,
> War sounds the trump, he rushes to the field . . .

Johnson's verses, which quickly became famous, appeared within Wolfe's life-time. Long after it, and writing of the year 1778, Boswell records the following incident concerning his hero:

We talked of war. JOHNSON: 'Every man thinks meanly of himself for not having been a soldier, or not having been at sea.' BOSWELL: 'Lord Mansfield does not.' JOHNSON: 'Sir, if Lord Mansfield were in a company of General Officers and Admirals who have been in service, he would shrink; he'd wish to creep under the table.' BOSWELL: 'No; he'd think he could *try* them all.' JOHNSON: 'Yes, if he could catch them: but they'd try him much sooner. No, Sir; were Socrates and Charles the Twelfth of Sweden both present in any company, and Socrates to say, 'Follow me, and hear a lecture in philosophy' and Charles, laying his hand on his sword, to say: 'Follow me, and dethrone the Czar' a man would be ashamed to follow Socrates. Sir, the impression is universal; yet it is strange.

Strange even to Johnson, stranger today, but never strange to Wolfe. For above all else, he kept steadily before him an ideal of personal conduct, and one which never altered. It was first expressed in a letter to his father written from Scotland in the course of peace-time duty. 'Few men,' he wrote, 'are acquainted with the degrees of their own courage till danger proves them, and they are seldom justly informed how far the love of honour or dread of shame are superior to the love of life.' A soldier's aim was to win battles, and, he said, 'a battle gained is, I believe, the highest joy mankind is capable of receiving, to him who commands, and his merit must be equal to his success if it works no change to his disadvantage.'

The meaning in the last words is two-fold. Generals should not get swollen head, and it should also be noted that Wolfe already knew, from observation in battle, that it was not the mere winning of success which was important. The virtue lay in the follow-through. There, only the greater commanders had proved able to sustain the necessary momentum in the face of exhaustion, loss, and inevitable disorganisation.

Wolfe amplified these remarks, which were made early in his life, by words to his mother, written in 1755, which must have warmed her heart. She was in pain from rheumatism, and Wolfe was most concerned for her well-being.

I wish I could say anything that could comfort you, or advise anything that would do you good. I know you would be content with a little share of health, and for my part I have nothing to ask but just as much resolution as fits a soldier. For riches, honours, possessions, and the dazzling advantages of this world, I disregard them; my utmost desire and ambition is to look steadily upon danger, and the greatest happiness I wish for here is to see you happy.

Wolfe did not live to see his mother happy, if that suffering creature could ever have been capable of such a condition, but he could surely have felt that his own life and professional career had been fulfilled far beyond expectation. For a man who died at the age of thirty-two, he had achieved much, and always with his whole heart and strength. Such was his acute objectivity, even about himself, that it would have caused him some of that wry amusement so often noted by his friends to note that he had

Bust of Wolfe by Wilton

become a national hero. What he had done he had worked for, and if, at the last, luck had helped him, had he not himself always had an almost uncanny sense of what he called 'the lucky moment in war'?

One of Wolfe's literary contemporaries was William Collins, who died the same year as the general, and when not much older. To Collins, the Duke of Cumberland was a hero, and Culloden, where Wolfe had served, a blow in freedom's cause. Our view of that event may have modified, but Collins was sincere enough when he wrote, of those who fell on the winning side of that battle:

> How sleep the Brave, who sink to rest
> By all their Country's wishes bless'd!

His poem ended:

> There Honour comes, a pilgrim gray
> To bless the turf that wraps their clay;
> And Freedom shall a while repair
> To dwell a weeping hermit there.

In point of fact Wolfe for one, when his own turn came, was not permitted to sleep undisturbed, except in the most literal sense. His body had no sooner reached home than it was viewed by curious eyes, while his reputation became a matter of such controversy that Townshend, suspecting Albemarle to have been the author of anonymous attacks on him for, as it would have appeared, denigrating the general, actually challenged his fellow officer to a duel. This was prevented by direct order of the King.

Wolfe's precise stature has offered a lively subject ever since to the military historian and commentator. A fair verdict seems to be that he was indifferent as a strategist, good as a tactician, and superlative as a personal leader and trainer of regular infantry. There is no guessing what further feats he might have achieved had he lived, but every indication that he felt he would not live long. At Quebec a sense of doom oppressed him, yet this was only a deepening of the premonition he had had for years.

If 'Honour came, a pilgrim gray,' to attend his obsequies, Freedom must surely have been an absentee, since whatever Wolfe died for, it was not in her cause. New France was no threat to his own country, whatever it may once have been to the Colonies of New England. It was quite the other way about, and it is ironical that he and Montcalm, so similar in their fate, should have been enlisted to support the cause of Canadian unity. Neither soldier gave much thought to the long-term future of Canada; they were there to do a particular job, Montcalm to defend, Wolfe to attack.

The acquisition of Canada by Great Britain, which was the direct result of the campaigns of Wolfe and Amherst, was not of unmixed advantage to the inhabitants, in spite of the enhanced interest which Britain took in the country compared with that of the France to which her people had looked heretofore. Indeed, some of the problems involved are still, after more than two centuries, unresolved. In this respect it is appropriate to quote words from M. Guy Frégault, the latest and one of the best historians of the earlier Canada, and the biographer of Vaudreuil. 'The framework of the Canadian community, destroyed in the crisis, was never rebuilt.' This states the case concisely, but perhaps with undue pessimism. What cannot be gainsaid is that Wolfe played a large part in the crisis. His statue stands at Quebec with that of Montcalm, and it is right that this should be so, for it serves to remind Canadians and their visitors that the two were brave men, and that they had respect for one another, even if matters greater than soldiering were beyond their scope.

As for the land where they died, it is impossible not to be uplifted by its splendour, its majestic scale, and its vast possibilities. Canada is a country whose resources, human and material are such that its future holds infinite promise. French and English have contributed much to its history, and the best among them may have built better and surer, perhaps much better, than is realised. The story of those adventurous spirits who are an essential part of the nation's legend has proved inspiriting to more than one generation – and this is surely as it should be. For if the age we live in may seem ultra-sophisticated and cynical, this is partly illusion. Certainly nothing is likely to diminish the pleasure of those for whom history is a vivid panorama rather than a forest of statistics illustrating a series of trends. As Thucydides said of the men he thought of as heroes: 'their story is not graven only on stone over their clay, but abides everywhere, without visible symbol, woven into the stuff of other men's lives.'

APPENDICES

I. POST-SCRIPT:
HAVANA AND MANILA

ALL was not over for Wolfe's army with the capture of Quebec. Murray and the troops were left to face a hard winter within the battered walls. In the early months of 1760 de Lévis, by a skilful and sustained attack on the garrison which had been weakened by cold, scurvy and limited supplies, very nearly reversed the victory of the previous year. For a time it was touch and go. Murray, short of fit men as he was, made a sortie in the confident expectation that the French would not stand against him: but they did so, and he was defeated outside the walls of the city, and driven back within it. Even to hold on to Quebec then seemed to depend upon whether French or British naval forces would be first up the St. Lawrence.

There was consternation when the news of Murray's reverse came through to London. 'Who the deuce', wrote Walpole, 'was thinking of Quebec? America was like a book one has read and done with, and here we are on a sudden reading our book backwards!' In the end, alarm died down, for it was the familiar frigate *Lowestoft* whose topsails were first sighted from the walls. She was followed within a week by the *Vanguard*, ship of the line, and by a second frigate. de Lévis thereupon gave up and stole away, leaving his siege guns behind him. He had felt able to cope with Murray, and had shown that he could do so; Murray and the British Navy were another matter.

'Join, my love, with me,' wrote Pitt to his wife Hester, 'in most humble and grateful thanks to the Almighty. The siege of Quebec was decided on May 17, with every happy circumstance... Happy, happy day! My joy and hurry are inexpressable.' The 'hurry' was so that the great war Minister might press his advantage. Murray, with his by now much reduced force, was soon ready to advance up the river to join at last with Amherst. The army Wolfe had led took its due part in the final operations which secured Montreal, and ensured the conquest of Canada.

Any further exploits by his soldiers would have gratified Wolfe, and one of the matters which would most have concerned him would have been that his career should have had some direct impact on his profession. In a very real sense this was so. For when Horace Walpole had written, in that golden autumn of 1759, 'one would think we had plundered the East and West Indies of sunshine' he was all unknowingly being prophetic. These particular quarters of the globe were indeed to come under toll, and largely as a result of the success of the combined operations at Quebec. They were attacked three years later. The expeditions took some little time to materialise, but in due course, in the year 1762, they were sent to Havana in the West Indies and Manila in the East. The opportunity arose because Spain joined France in the war against Britain and, as always, she was vulnerable overseas.

When the operations were planned, Pitt was out of office, and there was a new King who did not favour him, but something of the Minister's urgent spirit was alive in the Government, and Anson was still at the Admiralty, though he was then in the last months of his life. The expeditions were entirely independent, but as it happened they were almost concurrent, and they were agreed upon in principle at the same meeting of the Secret Committee which reviewed and decided war plans.

Devonshire, Anson, Ligonier, Grenville, Newcastle, Bute and Egremont were present. 'We began,' wrote Newcastle, 'with my lord Anson's project for attacking Havana, and after hearing the facility with which his lordship and Lord Ligonier apprehended there was in doing it, we all unanimously ordered the undertaking.' Newcastle was no thruster, but if a task seemed easy, if there were forces available to carry it out, and if, above all, it was likely to reflect credit on those in office, his vote would not be with-held.

No sooner was the matter settled than Lord Egremont brought forward a project submitted by a Colonel William Draper for taking Manila with troops and ships already in the Far East, and in concert with the East India Company. This was also 'in a manner' agreed to, though much more tentatively. The scene was remote, and success would depend upon factors unknown to London. There were sound reasons favouring both enterprises. Havana was the centre of Spanish power in the Caribbean. An attack on Manila, so it was thought, would hinder the Spanish in the Philippines from interfering with the growing British trade with Canton, of which Anson, as a result of his famous voyage during the previous war, had special knowledge.

Ingredients in common with Quebec were many, so far as Havana was concerned, and this was by far the more important episode of the two. It was in fact the largest expedition of its kind in the current struggle, involving 16,000 troops, a formidable fleet, and attendant transports. The general was Lord Albemarle, the admiral Sir George Pocock. Both men were well endowed before, but Havana brought them each a noble fortune. Albemarle was a soldier of limited capacity, and he did not enhance his military reputation. Pocock, who had done well as a Commander-in-Chief on the East India Station, left as little to be desired as fleet commander as had Saunders at Quebec.

As Lord Bury, Albemarle had at one time been Wolfe's colonel, but he was an absentee who annoyed Wolfe by refusing him badly needed leave of absence. He described Bury as 'one of those showy men who are seen in palaces and in the Courts of men . . . He desires never to see his Regiment, and wishes that no officer would ever leave it.' Wolfe was given no reason to modify his professional view of his colonel, yet in another way Bury could not have been kinder. For when, at last, Wolfe was given the freshener for which he pined, and went to Paris, Bury gave him a letter to his father, who was then British Ambassador. Wolfe wrote: 'Lord Albemarle has behaved to me in a manner that I could not presume to expect from him. Whenever he comes to Paris he immediately sends for me to his house and puts me upon so easy and genteel a footing that I have not language enough to return him proper thanks.'

Lord Bury succeeded to his father's earldom in 1754, and eight years later, as a protegé of the Duke of Cumberland, who was then in favour with his nephew, the young George III, he was ripe for a lucrative command. With him to Havana went two of his brothers, Major General the Hon. William Keppel and Commodore the Hon. Augustus Keppel, their presence making triply certain of the family fortunes. Commodore Keppel was second to Pocock, and among the post-captains was Augustus Hervey, who, as always, did brilliantly in the naval line. The ships present included the *Alcide, Centurion, Devonshire, Namur, Pembroke, Porcupine, Richmond, Stirling Castle, Sutherland* and others which had been with Saunders in the St. Lawrence.

It was among the higher ranks of the army that the affinities with Quebec were most striking. Patrick Mackellar was there as Chief Engineer, so was Colonel Howe, so was Colonel Carleton, in charge of Light Infantry and Grenadiers and so, at a later stage, was Brigadier Ralph Burton, who was sent by Amherst with a contingent from America. And it was from Martinique, where he found Monckton consolidating the gains he had made from the French (though he had had a slight difference with Rodney about sending reinforcements to Jamaica) that Albemarle wrote a private letter to Amherst, whom he addressed as 'Dear Jeff . . .' and with whom he used a mocking style which suggested that he had as yet no *rapport* with the soldiers he was to take into action, and of whom he wrote as if they had nothing to do with himself.

Your army is a fine one, brave to the last degree, almost spoilt by the expedition up the River St. Lawrence. Your officers are all generals, with a thorough contempt for anybody that has not served under *Mr Wolfe*: they either suffer, or cannot prevent, the soldiers doing what they please, which is the cause of great loss by sickness and the numbers falling down daily. I dare not find fault as yet but I am greatly afraid thay will oblige me to tell them my mind when we are better acquainted.

The troops of whom Albemarle thus spoke were, many of them, the same who had been at the Heights of Abraham. Every one of Wolfe's line regiments was present at Havana except for Fraser's Highlanders, and there was a contingent of Royal Americans and Rangers. Most of them had also served with distinction under Monckton at Martinique, and it was perhaps to have been expected that Albemarle should have been wary of them, considering their battle experience, and the fact, which he stressed to Amherst, that their fighting methods were unorthodox. Had his own been more so, Havana might have been won quicker.

Knowing from his own recollections of fighting the Spaniards of the Empire, and from the narratives of Drake's exploits in an earlier age which were his familiar reading, Anson realised the huge advantages to be gained by surprise in distant theatres of war. His idea was that Havana, which was towards the western end of the long island of Cuba, should be approached by the difficult and little-used Old Bahama Channel, on the north side. Thanks to a brilliant piece of surveying on the part of Captain John Elphinston of the frigate *Richmond*, Pocock's armada negotiated this safely, and was in sight of Havana before the Spaniards had taken any defensive steps.

The force arrived on 6 June and it was necessary to complete the conquest as soon as possible, for two cogent reasons. In all West Indian campaigning of those days, excessive heat and yellow fever took a tremendous toll of troops, far more than fighting. There was also the need for the fleet and transports to be clear of the area, or snug within a friendly harbour, by the end of August, the start of the hurricane season. Time was of the essence.

If Albemarle had shown outstanding imagination and initiative it is possible that Havana would have fallen more quickly, perhaps by a *coup de main*, but this would have meant lightning speed, and the army had not yet learnt the value of this. As it was, the very successful early landings did not bring particular advantages, and the general was soon pre-occupied, as was inevitable, with the reduction of El Morro, the great stronghold which stood on the east side of the land-locked harbour, whose entrance was protected by a boom.

The details of the ensuing campaign were complex, and the soldiers and sailors did all that could have been expected from them, thus belying Albemarle's early misgivings. William Howe and Carleton greatly distinguished themselves in action, as they had done at Quebec. Havana was well garrisoned, and with Pocock in such strength it was obviously the Governor's best policy to employ all his available naval resources ashore rather than afloat. This he did most effectively.

The soul of the garrison of El Morro was Captain Don

Luis de Velasco, who conducted such a magnificent defence
that it was the end of July before the fortress fell, by which time
Don Luis had been mortally wounded. He had emulated the
part of Montcalm, and he met with the same sad fate, to the
sorrow of friends and foes alike, who could not say too much for
his courage and skill. The city itself surrendered within a
fortnight, and it proved so rich that even in the first distribution
of prize-money the Commanders-in-Chief netted nearly
£70,000 apiece, and in the end they cleared double that sum,
an immense haul in the values of the day. As usual, the proceeds
were ridiculously unfair to the rank and file. A private soldier
got a princely £4–1–8½ and a bluejacket £3–14–9¾.

So prolonged had been the Spanish defence that the city was
taken only just in time before sickness began to take an intolerable toll. Even as it was the army lost 658 men in action as
against 4,708 from fever, naval figures showing comparable
proportions. Those who survived were often wrecks, and the
hospitals were soon full of invalids. Even Albermarle did not
escape. He lived for ten more years, but was never the same man
afterwards.

In his official despatch, Pocock's reference to the harmony
between the Services was even stronger than the terms employed
by Saunders after Quebec.

It will be needless, (he wrote) almost impossible for me to express or
describe that perfect harmony that has uninterruptedly subsisted
between the Fleet and Army from our first setting out. Indeed it is
doing injustice to both to mention them as two Corps, since each
has endeavoured, with the most constant and cheerful emulation, to
render it but one, uniting in the same principles of Honour and Glory
for their King and Country's service.

There was nothing so gruelling as the taking of El Morro at
Manila. The forces were launched from Madras in August 1762,
Colonel Draper, the originator and commander, having been
appointed a local Brigadier. The ships were in charge of Rear
Admiral Samuel Cornish, a man who had risen from the lower
deck by sheer ability. In comparison with Havana it was all on
a miniature scale, and the one direct link with Quebec was the
fact that the frigate *Seahorse*, in which Nelson was later to serve,

was in both expeditions. As at Havana, complete surprise was achieved, but the follow up in the Philippines was incomparably easier, and the siege was conducted in exemplary fashion. Close co-operation between army and navy, careful advance plans for the landing procedures, sterling work on the stowing arrangements, which were always so important in combined operations, and an almost incredible speed in execution, produced a highly satisfactory result, of which little was made either in England or even in India.

The acquisition proved to be of small value to Britain, and, except for a single galleon which was taken in prize, of almost as little to the senior commanders. Manila was hard to govern, and two years later, the place having been returned to Spain under a clause of the peace agreement, the garrison was glad enough to hand over to a resistance force which was in control of large areas outside the capital. The Spaniards had trouble in re-establishing their authority, though eventually they did so.

Manila is almost a forgotten episode, and the Philippines have so long been associated with the United States that even professional American historians are sometimes hesitant to credit that there was a British occupying force in the islands well over two centuries ago. But the evidence admits of no doubt, and the whole affair was conducted on the pattern set by Saunders and Wolfe. Naval and military co-operation had progressed a long way since the time of Rochefort, and it was Quebec which had shown the way.

II. REGIMENTS AT QUEBEC

THE direct descendants of regiments which stood in line of battle at the Heights of Abraham on 13 September 1759 have QUEBEC among their battle-honours, also MARTINIQUE and HAVANA.

> 15th Foot, now the Prince of Wales's Own Regiment of Yorkshire
> 28th Foot, now the Gloucestershire Regiment
> 35th Foot, now the 3rd Battalion, the Queens Regiment
> 43rd Foot, now the 1st Battalion, Royal Green Jackets
> 47th Foot, now the Queen's Lancashire Regiment
> 48th Foot ⎞
> 58th Foot ⎠ now the 2nd Battalion, Royal Anglians
> Royal Americans, now the 2nd Battalion, Royal Green Jackets.

The Louisbourg Grenadiers and Howe's Light Infantry were temporary formations composed of companies drawn from other Regiments. These companies returned to their parent regiments with the ending of the war in North America. The 78th Highlanders was also a temporary regiment raised in 1756 and disbanded in 1763. It was raised again in 1778, becoming eventually the Seaforth Highlanders, but the Seaforth regiment, with its own honourable traditions, had no direct connection with the unit which served at Quebec.

III. SELECT BIBLIOGRAPHY

The Life of Major-General James Wolfe, by Robert Wright (1864).

Montcalm and Wolfe, by Francis Parkman (1884).

Collection des Manuscrits du Maréchal de Lévis, edited by H-R. Casgrain 12 vols (1889–1895).

Journal des Campagnes au Canada de 1755 à 1760, by Lt. Gen. le Comte de Maurés de Malartic (1890).

Wolfe, by A. G. Bradley (1895).

The Siege of Quebec and the Battle of the Plains of Abraham, by A. G. Doughty and G. W. Parmelee. 6 Vols. (1901).

England and the Seven Years War, by Julian Corbett 2 Vols. (1907).

The Logs of the Conquest of Canada, edited by William Wood (1909).

The Life and Letters of James Wolfe, by Beckles Willson (1909).

An Historical Journal of the Campaigns in North America, by Captain John Knox. First published 1769: edition by A. G. Doughty. 3 Vols. (1914–1916).

Wolfe and the Artists, by J. Clarence Webster (1924).

James Wolfe, Man and Soldier, by W. T. Waugh (1928).

Wolfe and North America, by F. E. Whitton (1929).

Le Grand Marquis: Pierre de Rigaud de Vaudreuil et la Louisiane, by Guy Frégault (1952).

Wolfe: Portraiture and Genealogy: Quebec House Advisory Committee (1959).

Quebec, 1759, The Siege and the Battle, by C. P. Stacey (1959).

The Capture of Quebec, by Christopher Lloyd (1959).

Wolfe at Quebec, by Christopher Hibbert (1959).

The Rest to Fortune, by Robin Reilly (1960).

Mad, is he? The Character and Achievement of James Wolfe, by Duncan Grinnell-Milne (1963).

Canada: The War of the Conquest, by Guy Frégault. Translated by Margaret M. Cameron (1969).

IV. ACKNOWLEDGEMENTS

The Siege of Quebec is very fully documented, and rigorous study continues. Outstandingly the best modern military appraisal is Colonel C. P. Stacey's *Quebec: the Siege and the Battle* (1959), to which authority the present work owes guidance which is gratefully acknowledged. Also most valuable are Professor Christopher Lloyd's *The Capture of Quebec* (1959) and Monsieur Guy Frégault's *Canada: the War of the Conquest* (1969). Thanks are due to the Public Record Office of Northern Ireland for leave to make use of manuscript material (D 162/77 B) which has not hitherto been drawn upon in a published work; to the Hon. David Erskine, for permission to use passages from his valuable edition of Augustus Hervey's *Journal* (1953); to Mr Richard Akehurst, for expert advice on the 18th century musket; to Mrs Howard Vyse, for secretarial work; and to Mr Charles Warner for enquiry into the climatic conditions of 18th century Canada. He and the writer happen to be descendants of Colonel John Hale, of the 47th Foot, who brought back news of Quebec to Pitt in London.

With regard to the combined operations which were so remarkable a consequence of Wolfe's last campaign, Professor David Syrett's *The Siege and Capture of Havana* (Navy Records Society: 1970) is of great value, as is Mr Nicholas Tracy's *The Capture of Manila* (The Mariner's Mirror: Vol. 55: 1969). Separate reference is made to the courtesies which have made the illustration of this work a special pleasure.

O.W.

V. A NOTE ON THE ILLUSTRATIONS

The annalist of Wolfe, well off as he is for illustrative material of a general kind, is less so in the matter of portraiture. Before personal dislike had warped his vision, Townshend had discovered Wolfe to be a good subject for the artist, with a face full of eagerness and character. Now that Wolfe was recognised as a national hero, artists sought material on which to work, not only for the Abbey monument, but for the satisfaction of thousands who wished to possess a 'likeness.'

There were difficulties. They arose from the fact that Wolfe had only once sat for a formal portrait, and this when he was a boy. The picture, which was in his mother's possession and was later acquired by the Warde family, was undistinguished, and as it was almost full face it would at best have been only of limited use to the sculptors. The name of the painter is not recorded, and in 1759 its very existence was known to few.

As the coloured Townshend drawing which Robert Wright, Wolfe's early biographer, found so convincing, was not then available, it was a spontaneous little sketch by Harvey Smyth, an ADC, which had to serve as a starting point for what was to develop into a thriving industry. It was lucky that Smyth's sketch (or, if it was not his own work, the sketch which he acquired at Quebec and which was ever afterwards attributed to him), was so vivid. When Richard Houston engraved it, General Warde exclaimed that it was 'the most life like thing ever done of him!' Indeed one of the small miracles about Wolfe is that out of such slender material, so much was made. To say that some of it is fiction is to miss the point, for the fiction became a separate matter. The fact is that, from surviving scraps, it is possible to know something of what Wolfe was like, or at least to realise his attraction.

Wilton, with his disappointing glimpse of the hero embalmed and coffined, was next after Smyth in the field. In addition to his preparatory work for the official monument, he made models, and of these at least one notable version survives. The Duke of Richmond, who commissioned it, may also have commissioned a painting by

J. S. C. Schaak, posthumous but at least near-contemporary, which served as a basic for a whole series of prints.

There were at least two designs for a monument other than Wilton's, one later and one earlier. The later example appeared in the *Gentleman's Magazine* in 1789 and came from the studio of Roubiliac, but it is conventional and disappointing. The earlier, though a mockery, is in its way a considerable oddity. It is unsigned, and it is without question the work of an amateur. From its tone the idea could have been Townshend's. At the top is the legend 'A LIVING DOG IS BETTER THAN A DEAD LION.' Then there is a pediment, within which is a grotesque roundel of Wolfe, facing right. Beneath are slightly misquoted lines from *Julius Caesar*:

> Set Honour in one Eye and Death in T'other
> And I will look on both indifferent
> And let the Gods so speed me as I love
> The name of Honour more than I fear Death.

Underneath the monument is the corpse of a dead lion, inscribed 'Here Lies Honour'. Against this animal a dog, with a collar inscribed 'MINDEN', rudely lifts its leg. The dog is given a two line jingle, inserted within a balloon, which is an adaptation of the well-known lines on Gay's monument in Westminster Abbey:

> Honour's a jest, and all things show it
> I thought so once, and now I know it.

The sting in the word 'Minden' is sharp. For although the British infantry had done magnificently in that battle, including the 20th Regiment, which Wolfe had trained, and which had the heaviest casualties among the six 'Minden' battalions, it led to a court-martial on Lord George Sackville for his failure to pursue the French with the cavalry under his command, in spite of repeated orders from Prince Ferdinand of Brunswick. Sackville was declared unfit to serve in any military capacity, his name being removed from the list of the Privy Council. He was well known to Wolfe, with whom he corresponded. In the course of time he assumed the name of Germain and staged a political come back, being largely responsible, as Secretary of State for the Colonies, for the disastrous course of the War of American Independence.

Whoever engraved the design thought it worth while to have a few copies printed off in sepia. There is an inscription: 'Published according to Act of Parliament', and at the bottom is:

THE VANITY OF HUMAN GLORY
A Design for the Monument to General Wolfe, 1760.

The thing was done when the country was still ringing with Wolfe's praise, and must have caused deep offence if any of his friends saw it, even though its barb was directed against Sackville. The best argument against it being by Townshend is that it is not amusing, as his cartoons almost invariably were.

Four years after Wolfe was buried, the young George Romney submitted a canvas, 'The Death of Wolfe' to the Free Society of Artists. Not much is known about it, except that it was thought good enough to get Romney an award. The painting had disappeared and no account of it survives, but it is likely that the figures appeared in classical dress, as was the convention of the time.

The next aspirant was Edward Penny, a considerable man in the art world of his day, a foundation member of the Royal Academy, and for some years its Professor of Painting. Penny did various versions of 'The Death of Wolfe' which in their quiet way have both interest and merit, for although the artist's attempt to render the physiognamy of the general is not likely to have been based on anything authentic, he went to much trouble to get the details of the scene as accurate as possible (see p. 169). The most realistic, now in a private collection, shows the dying hero lying on the ground supported by a soldier kneeling behind him. On Wolfe's right is another, wiping the general's face. Possibly this is Hewit, a surgeon's mate, who seems to have been at hand. Behind him stands a second soldier pointing towards the scene of battle. On the left a runner, waving his hat, approaches the group, announcing victory. It is based on information from Volunteer Henderson of the Louisbourg Grenadiers.

Penny's work was shown in 1764 at the Society of Artists but, perhaps from its very modesty, it created no stir. A rather less realistic version is now at the Ashmolean Museum, Oxford. It is signed and dated the year before the original exhibit and is slightly larger. It was given by the artist to the University in 1787. An element of fiction is introduced, though it is confined to the background. The central group is the same, but Penny, feeling perhaps that some suggestion was required that others besides Wolfe and the Grenadiers were involved, filled the background with a mass of soldiers, and on the right introduced sailors, and what are possibly intended as French prisoners. Over all hangs the smoke of battle, with Quebec in the left distance. Even with its more dramatic elements, Penny's Ashmolean picture is

West's boyhood of Wolfe

still unpretentious, and it would probably have been approved by most of those who had actually been present on the field.

Whatever participants may have thought, and they could at best have been but a tiny proportion of the potential public, there was one young man who looked upon Penny's efforts as very poor stuff in relation to the possibilities of the theme. This was Benjamin West. Born in America of Quaker stock, West had been discovered to be an infant prodigy as an artist. He had gone to Italy to learn something of his profession, thence to England to practise it. He had got a long way on the upward path by 1764, when he was still in his mid-twenties, and he was one day to follow Reynolds as President of the Royal Academy. His talents were moderate, but they were exactly suited to the taste of his time.

West was what was called a 'history Painter'; that is to say he would embark on large compositions with subjects such as 'Agrippina

Landing at Brindisi', or 'The Final Departure of Regulus from Rome', which country gentlemen, and public institutions, bought to furnish their galleries. But it was by portraiture that most artists lived, and it so happened that in 1764 West was asked to portray Monckton, the picture to be exhibited at the Society of Artists.

Since Quebec, Monckton had taken a leading part in combined operations against the French in Martinique, in which his naval counter-part had been Rodney. They had been successful, though the affair had not involved any very gruelling fighting. Although not a national figure, Monckton would have been of particular interest to West, since so much of his career had been spent on the far side of the Atlantic. And it would certainly have struck West, in conversation with him, that the battle for Quebec was, for an American, *the* high light of the Seven Years War. Amherst, for all his steady successes, had conducted nothing so breathtaking as the ascent to the Heights of Abraham. As neither Romney nor Penny had made much of a mark with their commemorations, the way seemed wide open for a major work on the subject.

West embarked on his canvas in 1770, full of energy and determined to succeed. His idea was to create a full-scale 'historical' picture, but with the difference that the people would appear in contemporary dress, not in the garb supposedly worn by the Ancients. It was true that Penny had taken the same line, but his work had been without the least pretension to 'grandeur.'

Reynolds was well informed about the project, and he called on West one day to protest at the innovation proposed. 'The event', so West replied, 'happened in the year 1759, in a region of the world unknown to the Greeks and Romans, and at a period of time when no warriors who wore such a costume existed. The subject I have to represent is a great battle fought and won, and the same truth which gives law to the historian should rule the painter.' When the picture was finished. Reynolds said, in generous praise: 'he has treated the subject as it ought to be treated. I retract my objections. I foresee that this picture will not only become one of the most popular, but will occasion a revolution in art.'

Reynolds was right – righter than he could have realised when he spoke, for the picture carried West to a height of fame unmatched in his particular sphere (see p. 174–5). It was shown at the Royal Academy in 1771. The buyer was Lord Grosvenor and it would have been the King had not George III head objections to the costumes. When West told his Majesty that Reynolds, for one, had been converted, a copy, the same size as the original, was ordered for the Royal Collection. In the following year the artist was appointed Historical Painter to the Court. If he had been successful before, now he was triumphant.

Clothing apart, the painting had not the slightest grounding in literal truth, though West went to some trouble to paint Wolfe as convincingly as he could, and he was later to make some smaller studies, for the Warde family, based on material in their collection at Squerries, near Westerham, which had been known to Wolfe from childhood.

West was not a man to let any opportunity slip by, and he grouped round Wolfe a number of principal characters in the campaign, most of whom were by then on the ascendant in their various lines, and who would be gratified to see themselves included in an important picture, destined no doubt to survive for posterity. The sorrowing crowd round the dying hero included Monckton, Hervey Smyth, Barré, Colonel Williamson, William Howe and Lieutenant Browne. There was at least one figure who had no business anywhere near the scene. The surgeon of Penny's composition was replaced by a man who was recognised as Dr. Robert Adair, who was not even in America at the time! Another highly unsuitable inclusion was an Indian, who was placed immediately facing Wolfe, and who looked meditatively towards him. Perhaps the best excuse for the intrusion of a savage whom Wolfe would have viewed with aversion was the fact that it was an Indian who, in West's boyhood, had supplied him with his first pigments.

There were notable absentees. Townshend and Murray were among them, for obvious reasons. Another was Colonel John Hale. Rumour had it that he would have been there if he had offered the artist a consideration of £100. This may perhaps have been libel, and in any case Hale had helped to secure Wolfe's fame (and his own) in quite another way. As a reward for bringing home the Quebec despatch he was given the Colonelcy of one of five new cavalry regiments, the 18th Light Dragoons. For its crest Hale chose a skull and cross-bones, with the motto 'Glory'. The Regiment later became the 17th Lancers (the 'Death or Glory Boys') and it was present in the force commanded by William Howe at the battle of Bunker Hill, during the War of American Independence.

Monckton, the most friendly towards Wolfe of the three brigadiers, thought well enough of West's picture to order a full-size copy, and the engravers soon got busy with it. Penny's work had already had a modest second run as the basis for a print by Richard Houston, but it was nothing to the popularity which accrued to West as a result of the rendering of his work by William Woollett, which was marketed

Bow figurine of Wolfe

by John Boydell, an expert salesman and publicist who later became Lord Mayor of London. The print appeared in 1776. It had brought Boydell and West no less than £15,000 by the year 1790, being a runaway best seller from the start. It also brought Woollett the honour of appointment as 'Historical Engraver to His Majesty' and it helped to revolutionise the trade in prints.

Hitherto, France had been an exporter of prints to London on a large scale. As a result of West, Woollett and Boydell, though of course not solely on their account, there was soon an export revenue from this line of merchandise of some £200,000 a year. The French were in fact so taken with West's picture – after all, Wolfe had been struck down by a French bullet – that a Parisian craftsman, Justus Chevillet, produced a companion scene of the death of Montcalm after an original by Vateau. This was wilder than anything conceived in London. The general was shown dying on the field of battle, at which not just one but two Indian warriors were present. A feature of the background was a palm-tree, looking as if it was growing out of Montcalm's tent.

One other artist, James Barry, was moved to produce a version of the death of Wolfe as a rival to West's, but met with no success. If reproductions are a true guide, the work could be described as Penny livened up. Wolfe is seen half naked, with two Louisbourg Grenadiers attending him. A messenger is bringing news of the battle and on the left is what looks like a naval officer, in impeccable dress, and a sorrowing Highlander. Quebec burns in the background. Barry accepted the idea of contemporary attire, and he aimed to combine something of Penny's accuracy with West's sense of occasion. But the public swallowed West, and wanted no one else. They have accepted him ever since.

West provided a final link between Wolfe and Nelson, for he lived to memorialise Trafalgar, though by then he was rather in decline, and the theme was more successfully attended to by others. But a story was current about artist and admiral which was very much in character. The pair, it seems, met at a public dinner during one of Nelson's rare spells ashore. Nelson, by way of making conversation with West, who happened to be his neighbour, said how much he regretted he had not acquired a taste for art in his youth, as well as some discrimination. 'But', he added, 'there is one picture whose power I *do* feel. I never pass a print shop where your 'Death of Wolfe' is in the window without being stopped by it.' He asked why West had done no more like it. 'Because, my lord, there are no more subjects,' replied the painter. 'Damn it,' said Nelson, 'I didn't think of that!' He then asked West to take a glass of champagne, the wine he favoured. 'My lord,' so West is said to have continued, 'I fear that your intrepidity may yet furnish me with another such scene, and if it should, I shall certainly avail myself of it.' 'Will you?' asked Nelson eagerly, pouring out bumpers, '*will* you, Mr. West? Then I hope I die in the next battle!'

VI. LIST OF
ILLUSTRATIONS

Page numbers in bold type indicate illustrations in colour

after sketch by Captain Hervey Smyth, 1760. British Museum, London. *Photo R. B. Fleming & Co.*

56. View of Queen's Square, Bath. Aquatint by Thomas Malton, 1784. British Museum, London. *Photo Eileen Tweedy.*

57. Portrait of Katharine Lowther as the Duchess of Bolton by Richard Cosway. By kind permission of Lord Barnard, Raby Castle. *Photo Public Archives of Canada, Ottawa.*

59. Portrait of James Wolfe by Elizabeth, Duchess of Devonshire. National Portrait Gallery, London.

61. Portrait of Sir Charles Saunders by Joshua Reynolds, 1765. National Maritime Museum, London.

63. Portrait of James Cook by John Webber. Portrait of John Jervis, Earl of St Vincent by F. Cotes, 1769. National Portrait Gallery, London.

64. H.M.S. *Sutherland* by Richard Short. National Maritime Museum, London.

67. Portrait of Isaac Barré by G. Stuart. National Portrait Gallery, London. Portrait of Guy Carleton by an unknown artist, *c.* 1780. By kind permission of the Earl of Malmesbury.

70. Portrait of Pierre de Rigaud, Marquis de Vaudreuil Cavagnal by Henri Beau. The Public Archives of Canada, Ottawa.

71. Portrait of Louis-Joseph, Marquis de Montcalm-Gozon by an unknown artist. The Public Archives of Canada, Ottawa.

73. Soldier of Le Régiment de la Reine, 1759, by C. C. P. Lawson. National Trust, Quebec House, Westerham. *Photo Eileen Tweedy.*

74. View of the rue des Recolets, Quebec, before the siege. National Trust, Quebec House, Westerham. *Photo Eileen Tweedy.*

76. Portrait of Madame de Pompadour by François Boucher, 1758. Victoria and Albert Museum, London. *Photo Crown Copyright.*

77. Portrait of Louis XV in state robes by Carl van Loo. Versailles. *Photo Réunion des Musées Nationaux, Paris.*

78. Portrait of Count Louis-Antoine de Bougainville. Musée de la Marine, Paris.

86. Men of the Lancashire Militia by Edward Dayes. National Trust, Quebec House, Westerham. *Photos Eileen Tweedy.*

88. Mitre cap of the 43rd Regiment, 1740–49. National Army Museum.

89. Examples of the 'Brown Bess' musket. The Armouries, Tower of London. *Photo British Crown Copyright— reproduced with permission of the Controller of Her Britannic Majesty's Stationery Office.*

91. Portrait of Wolfe at Quebec, after a sketch by Captain Hervey Smyth, 1759. By kind permission of Major and Mrs. J. B. Warde. *Photo Eileen Tweedy.*

92. *Grenadiers of the 47th and 48th Regiments of Foot.* Detail from a painting by David Morier, 1751. Reproduced by gracious permission of Her Majesty the Queen.

96. Detail from Cook's manuscript chart of the St Lawrence. National Maritime Museum, London.

102–3. View of the city of Quebec, 1740. British Museum, London. *Photo R. B. Fleming & Co.*

104–5. View of the modern city of Quebec. *Photo Quebec House, London.*

107. Eighteenth century plan of Quebec. British Museum, London. *Photo R. B. Fleming & Co.*

109. Portrait of General Monckton. National Trust, Quebec House, Westerham. *Photo Eileen Tweedy.*

111. View of the Montmorency Falls. Engraving after sketch by Captain Hervey Smyth, 1759. National Army Museum.

115. View of the Church of Notre Dame, Quebec. Engraving after Richard Short, 1761. British Museum, London. *Photo Eileen Tweedy.*

116. 'Ah, Monsieur le General'. Cari-

INDEX

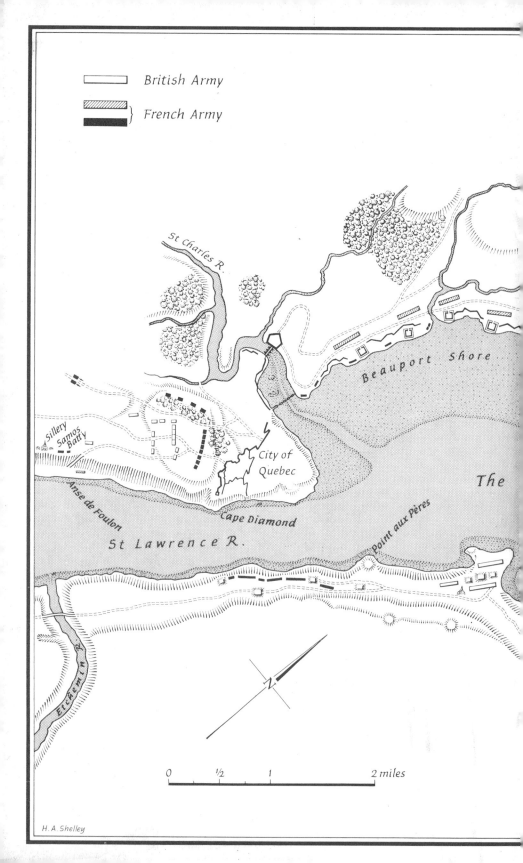

British Army

} French Army

St Charles R.

Beauport Shore

Sillery
Samos
Batty

City of
Quebec

Anse de Foulon

Cape Diamond

Point aux Pères

St Lawrence R.

The

Etchemin R.

N

0   ½   1   2 miles

H. A. Shelley